A WHO HQ GRAPHIC

Who Sparked the Montgomery Bus Boycott?

ROSA PARKS

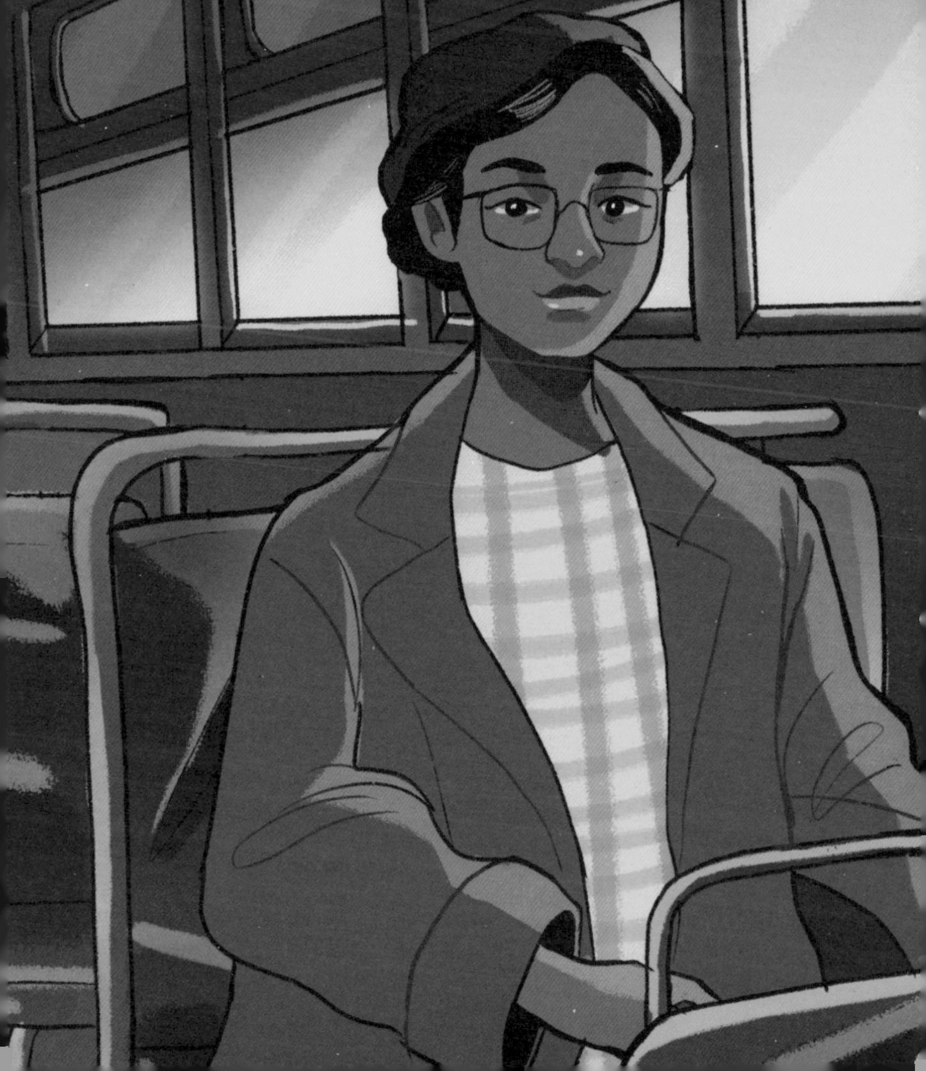

To my parents. To Rosa. Be humble. Be kind—IF

To my family, friends, and community—AH

PENGUIN WORKSHOP
An Imprint of Penguin Random House LLC, New York

Penguin supports copyright. Copyright fuels creativity, encourages diverse voices,
promotes free speech, and creates a vibrant culture. Thank you for buying an authorized
edition of this book and for complying with copyright laws by not reproducing, scanning,
or distributing any part of it in any form without permission. You are supporting writers
and allowing Penguin to continue to publish books for every reader.

The publisher does not have any control over and does not assume any responsibility for author
or third-party websites or their content.

Visit us online at www.penguinrandomhouse.com.

Library of Congress Cataloging-in-Publication Data is available upon request.

ISBN 9780593224465 (pbk)   10 9 8 7 6 5 4 3 2 1 HH
ISBN 9780593224472 (hc)   10 9 8 7 6 5 4 3 2 1 HH

Lettering by Comicraft
Book design by Jay Emmanuel

This is a work of nonfiction. All of the events that unfold in the narrative
are rooted in historical fact. Some dialogue and characters have been fictionalized
in order to illustrate or teach a historical point.

For more information about your favorite historical figures, places, and events,
please visit www.whohq.com

A WHO HQ GRAPHIC NOVEL

Who Sparked the Montgomery Bus Boycott?

ROSA PARKS

by Insha Fitzpatrick
illustrated by Abelle Hayford
colors by Hanna Schroy

Penguin Workshop

Introduction

Rosa Parks looked at her watch as she waited for the Cleveland Avenue bus at the corner of Montgomery and Moulton Streets in Montgomery, Alabama. It was Thursday, December 1, 1955, and forty-two-year-old Rosa wanted to go home after a long day of working as a seamstress. She'd been in Montgomery for twenty years, after spending her childhood on her grandparents' farm in Pine Level, Alabama, with her mother, Leona, and brother, Sylvester. But even though Montgomery was her home, she still didn't feel welcome there.

In the 1950s, Montgomery (and much of the American South) had unfair laws, known as Jim Crow laws. These laws made it so Black people were "separate but equal" from white people. There were a large number of places—including movie theaters, restaurants, churches, and even schools—where Black people could not go, or places they were separated from because of the color of their skin. Montgomery's bus system operated under these rules, and buses were divided into sections: a white section, a Black and white section, and a Black section. If a white passenger got on the bus and the bus was full, a Black passenger had to give up their seat for them.

As the Cleveland Avenue bus came to a halt, Rosa and the other passengers lined up to pay their fare. Rosa quickly boarded the bus and found a seat in the section meant for Black and white passengers. With every stop, the bus began to fill up. A few stops later, a white man stepped onto the bus, and the bus driver, James Blake, noticing there were no available seats, demanded that Rosa and three other Black passengers give up their seats and move to the back. As the three passengers began to move to the back, Rosa stayed seated.

Blake grew angrier by the second, his voice booming louder and louder. "Are you going to stand up?" Blake asked. Not moving an inch, Rosa looked straight at him and simply said, "No." "Well, I'm going to have you arrested," Blake barked. And Rosa, still sitting in her seat, calmly replied, "You may do that."

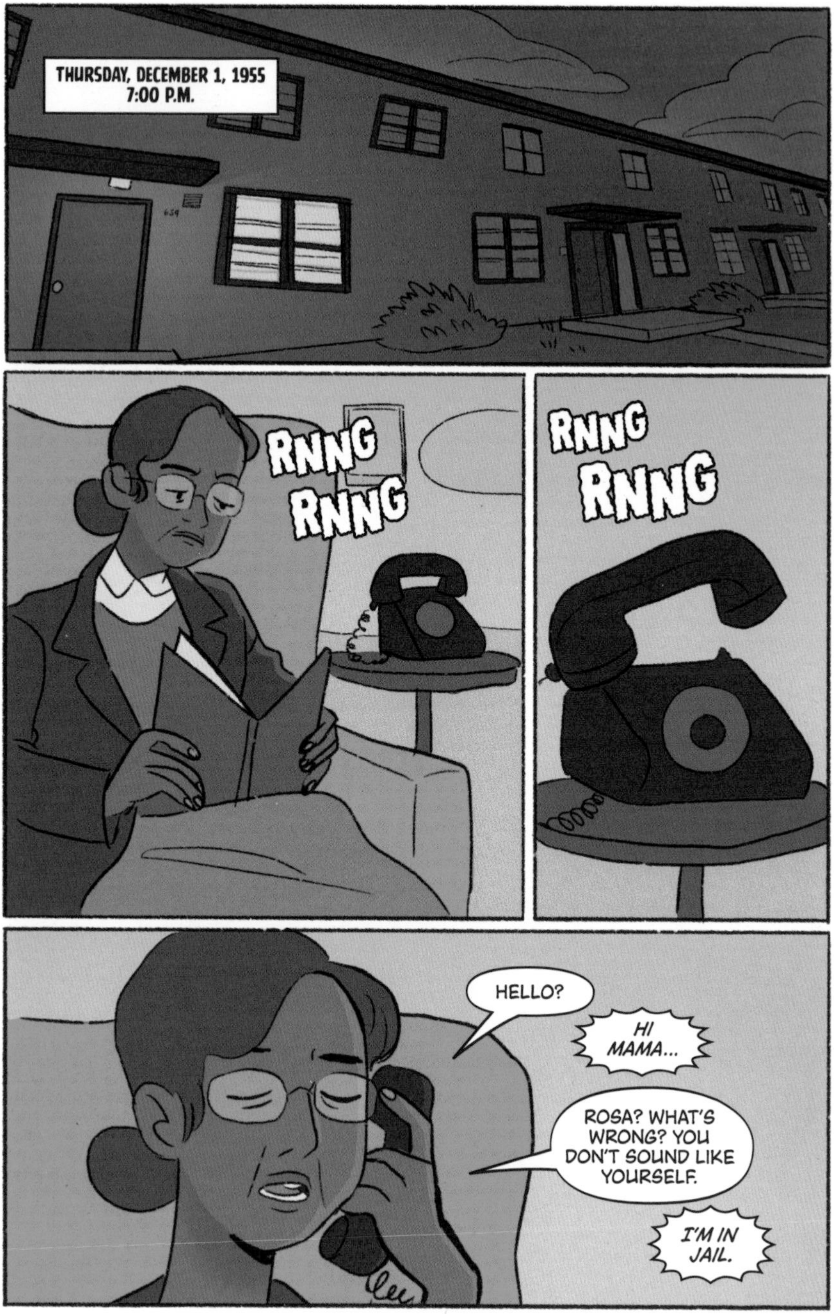
THURSDAY, DECEMBER 1, 1955
7:00 P.M.
RNNG
RNNG
RNNG
RNNG
HELLO?
HI MAMA...
ROSA? WHAT'S WRONG? YOU DON'T SOUND LIKE YOURSELF.
I'M IN JAIL.

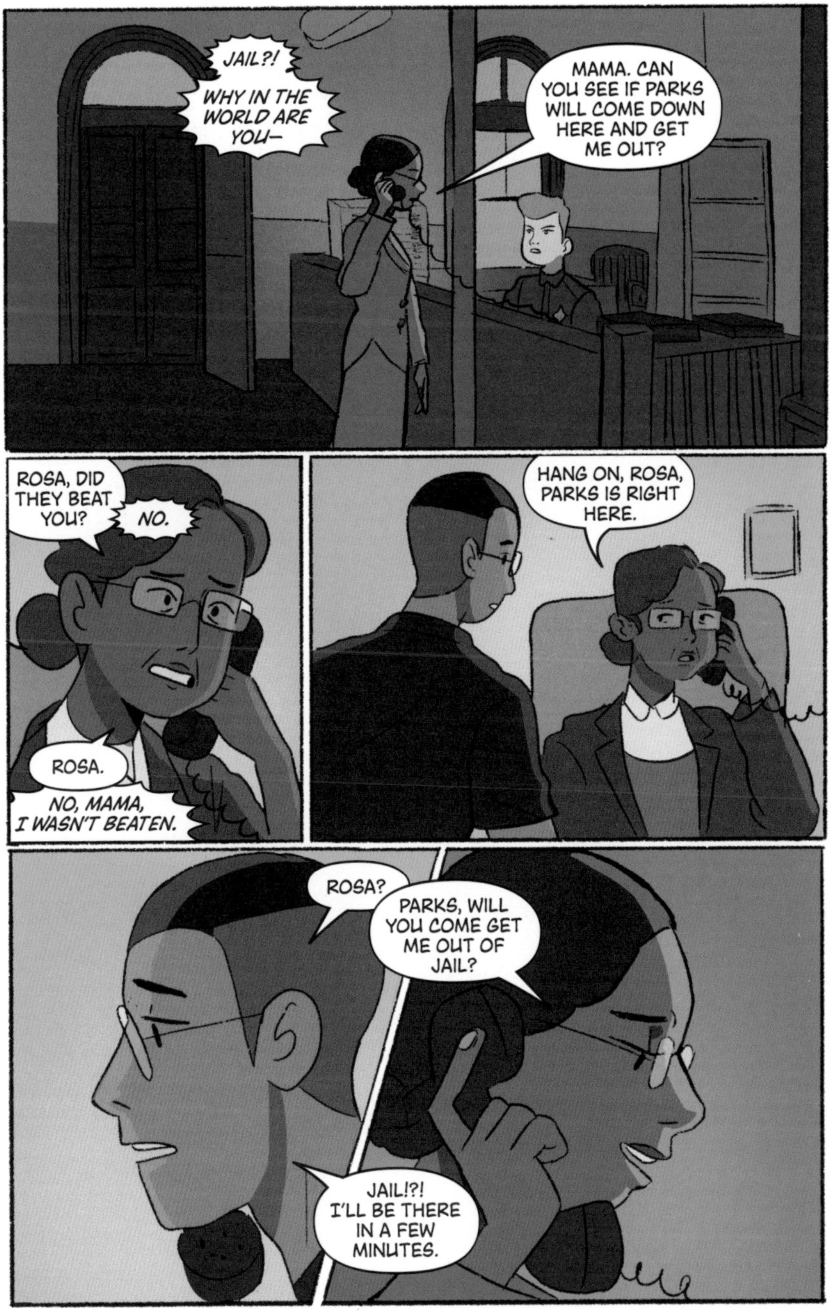
JAIL?!
WHY IN THE WORLD ARE YOU—
MAMA. CAN YOU SEE IF PARKS WILL COME DOWN HERE AND GET ME OUT?
ROSA, DID THEY BEAT YOU?
NO.
ROSA.
NO, MAMA, I WASN'T BEATEN.
HANG ON, ROSA, PARKS IS RIGHT HERE.
ROSA?
PARKS, WILL YOU COME GET ME OUT OF JAIL?
JAIL!?! I'LL BE THERE IN A FEW MINUTES.

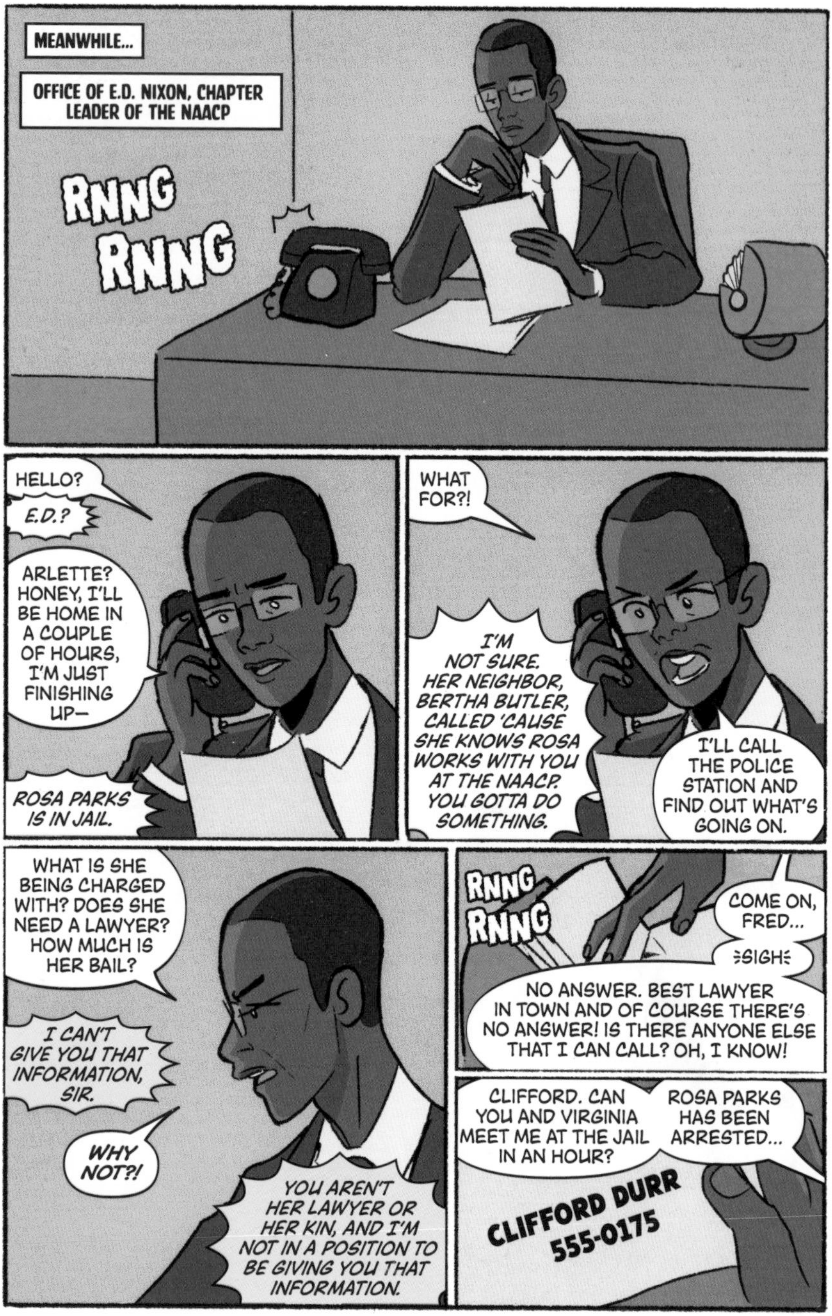
MEANWHILE...
OFFICE OF E.D. NIXON, CHAPTER LEADER OF THE NAACP
RNNG RNNG
HELLO?
E.D.?
ARLETTE? HONEY, I'LL BE HOME IN A COUPLE OF HOURS, I'M JUST FINISHING UP—
ROSA PARKS IS IN JAIL.
WHAT FOR?!
I'M NOT SURE. HER NEIGHBOR, BERTHA BUTLER, CALLED 'CAUSE SHE KNOWS ROSA WORKS WITH YOU AT THE NAACP. YOU GOTTA DO SOMETHING.
I'LL CALL THE POLICE STATION AND FIND OUT WHAT'S GOING ON.
WHAT IS SHE BEING CHARGED WITH? DOES SHE NEED A LAWYER? HOW MUCH IS HER BAIL?
I CAN'T GIVE YOU THAT INFORMATION, SIR.
WHY NOT?!
YOU AREN'T HER LAWYER OR HER KIN, AND I'M NOT IN A POSITION TO BE GIVING YOU THAT INFORMATION.
RNNG RNNG
COME ON, FRED...
SIGH
NO ANSWER. BEST LAWYER IN TOWN AND OF COURSE THERE'S NO ANSWER! IS THERE ANYONE ELSE THAT I CAN CALL? OH, I KNOW!
CLIFFORD. CAN YOU AND VIRGINIA MEET ME AT THE JAIL IN AN HOUR?
ROSA PARKS HAS BEEN ARRESTED...
CLIFFORD DURR 555-0175

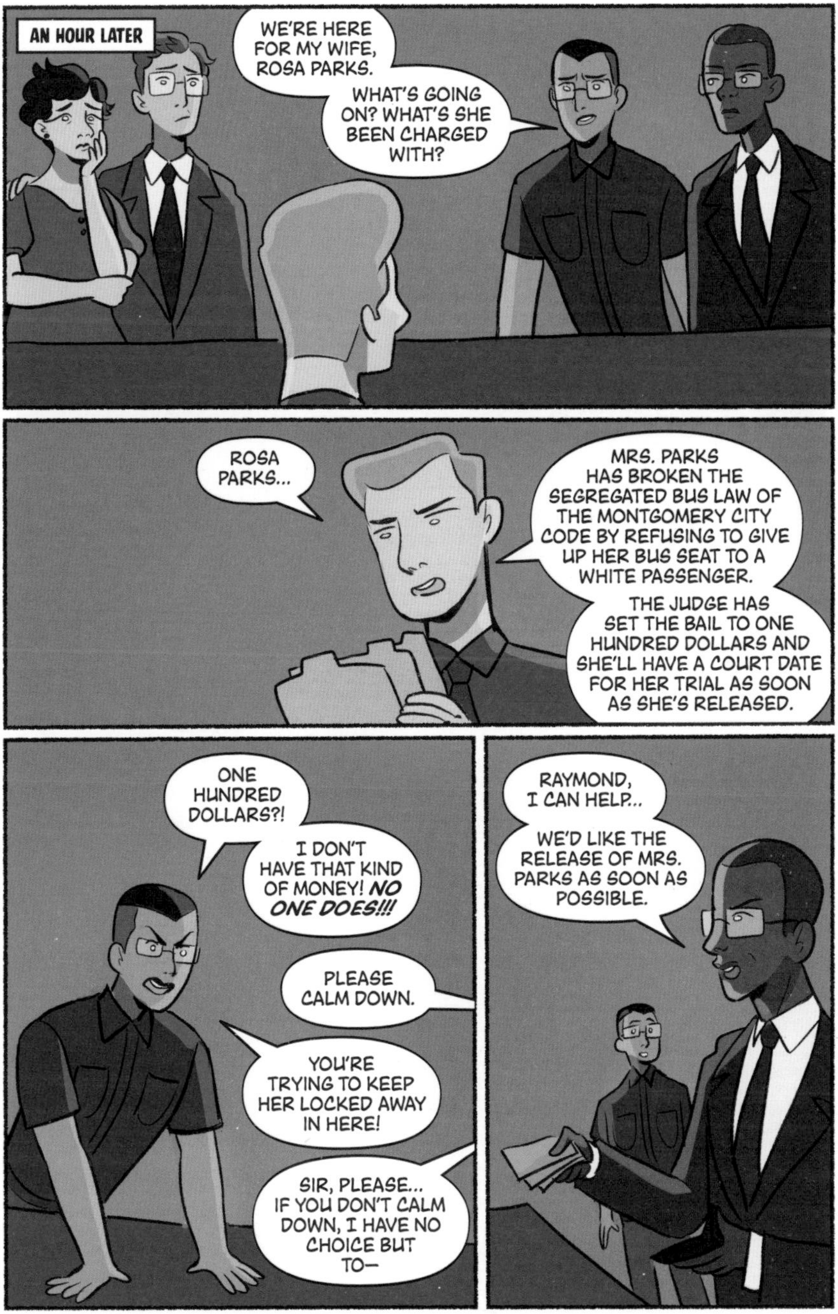
AN HOUR LATER
WE'RE HERE FOR MY WIFE, ROSA PARKS.
WHAT'S GOING ON? WHAT'S SHE BEEN CHARGED WITH?
ROSA PARKS...
MRS. PARKS HAS BROKEN THE SEGREGATED BUS LAW OF THE MONTGOMERY CITY CODE BY REFUSING TO GIVE UP HER BUS SEAT TO A WHITE PASSENGER.
THE JUDGE HAS SET THE BAIL TO ONE HUNDRED DOLLARS AND SHE'LL HAVE A COURT DATE FOR HER TRIAL AS SOON AS SHE'S RELEASED.
ONE HUNDRED DOLLARS?!
I DON'T HAVE THAT KIND OF MONEY! *NO ONE DOES!!!*
PLEASE CALM DOWN.
YOU'RE TRYING TO KEEP HER LOCKED AWAY IN HERE!
SIR, PLEASE... IF YOU DON'T CALM DOWN, I HAVE NO CHOICE BUT TO—
RAYMOND, I CAN HELP...
WE'D LIKE THE RELEASE OF MRS. PARKS AS SOON AS POSSIBLE.

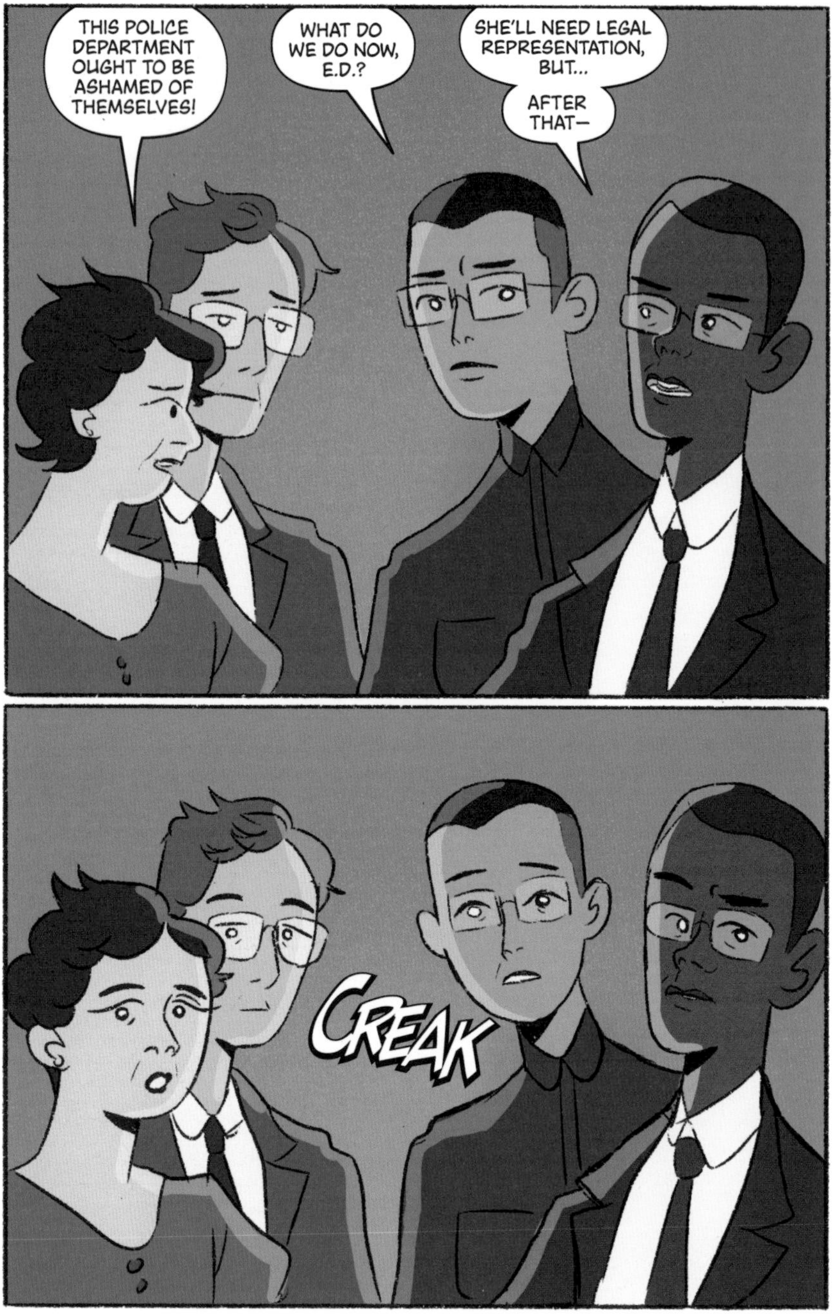
THIS POLICE DEPARTMENT OUGHT TO BE ASHAMED OF THEMSELVES!
WHAT DO WE DO NOW, E.D.?
SHE'LL NEED LEGAL REPRESENTATION, BUT...
AFTER THAT—
CREAK

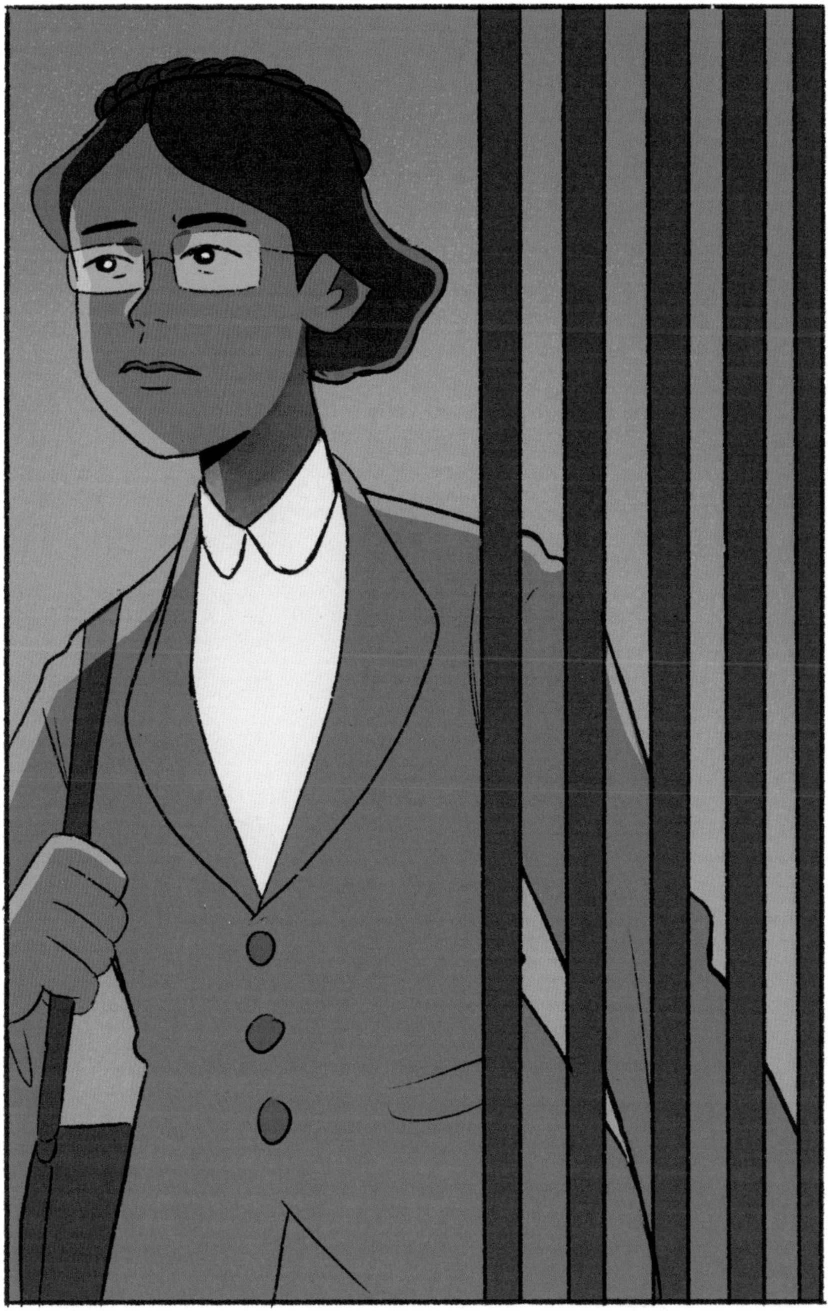

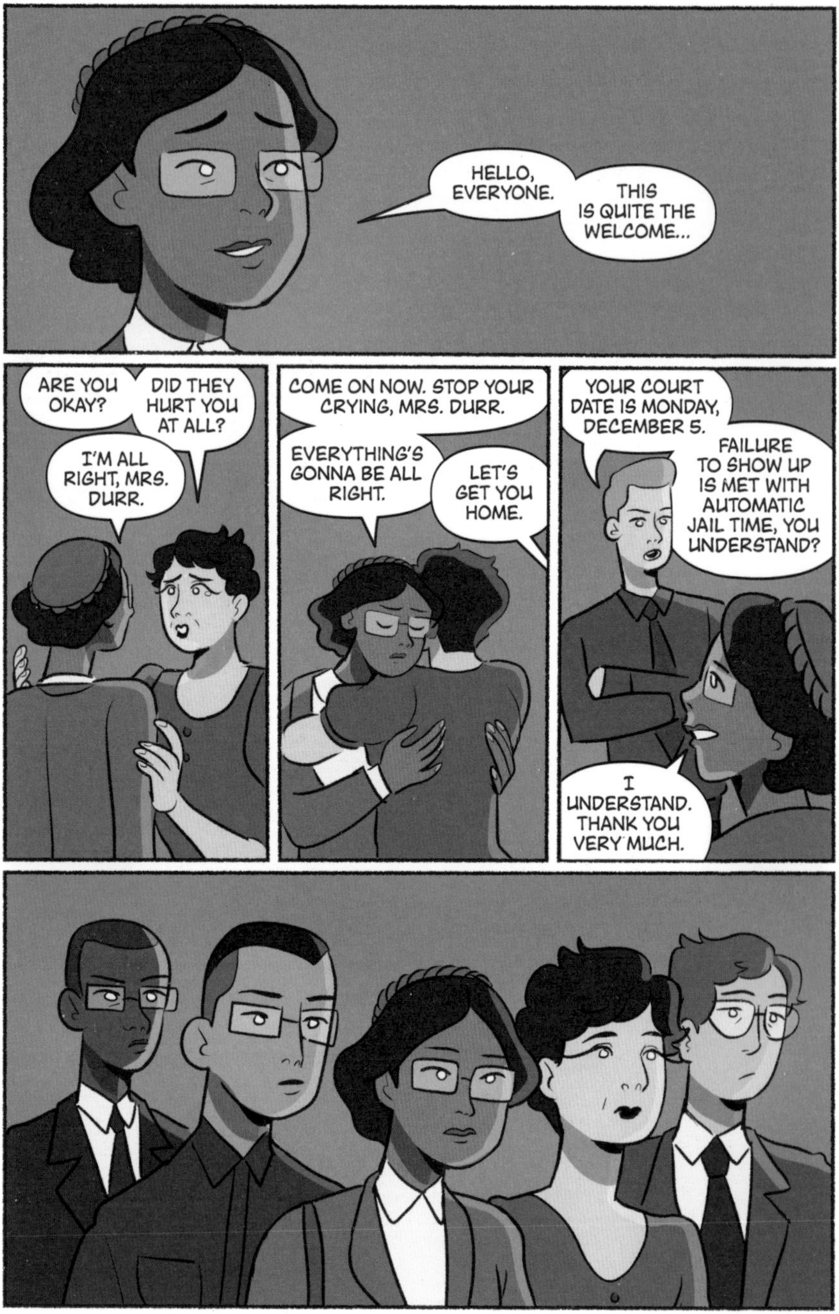
HELLO, EVERYONE.
THIS IS QUITE THE WELCOME...
ARE YOU OKAY?
DID THEY HURT YOU AT ALL?
I'M ALL RIGHT, MRS. DURR.
COME ON NOW. STOP YOUR CRYING, MRS. DURR.
EVERYTHING'S GONNA BE ALL RIGHT.
LET'S GET YOU HOME.
YOUR COURT DATE IS MONDAY, DECEMBER 5.
FAILURE TO SHOW UP IS MET WITH AUTOMATIC JAIL TIME, YOU UNDERSTAND?
I UNDERSTAND. THANK YOU VERY MUCH.

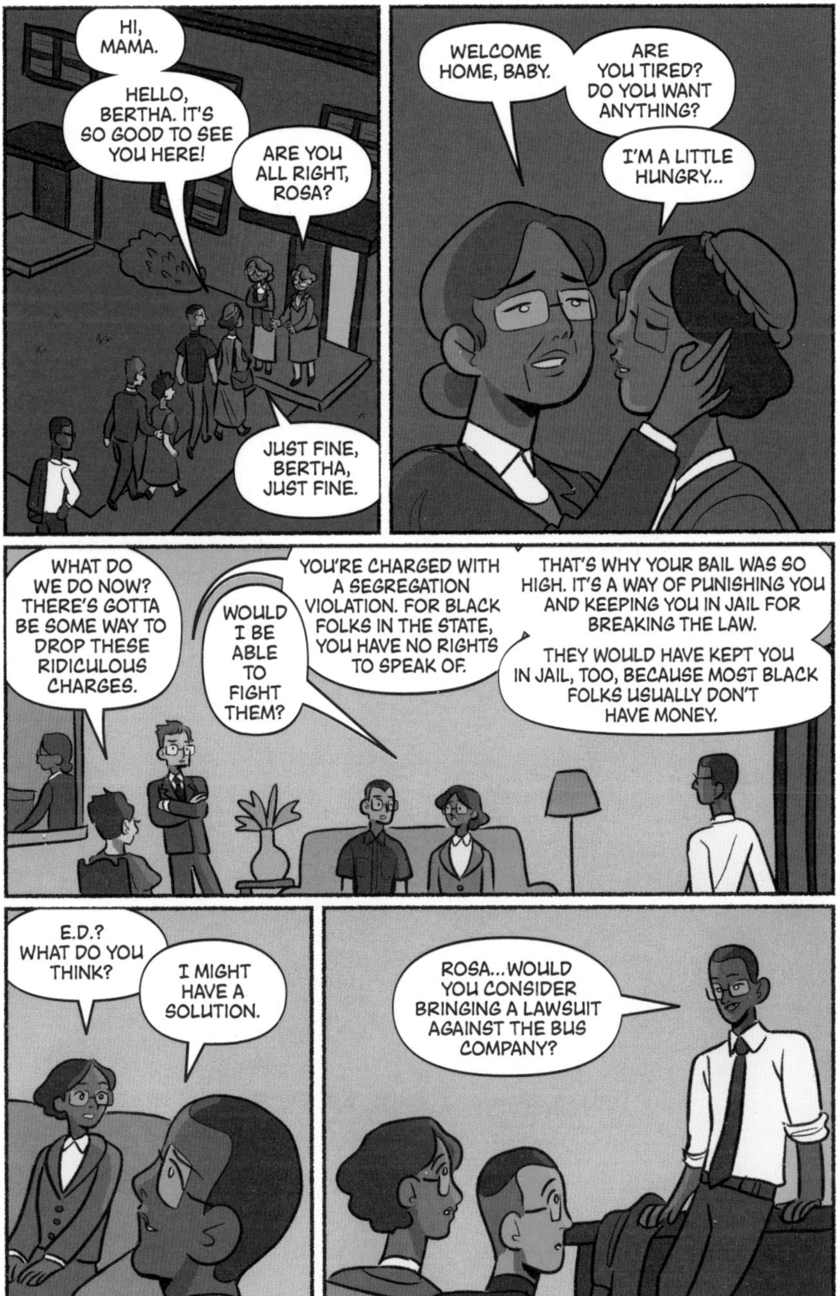
HI, MAMA.
HELLO, BERTHA. IT'S SO GOOD TO SEE YOU HERE!
ARE YOU ALL RIGHT, ROSA?
JUST FINE, BERTHA, JUST FINE.
WELCOME HOME, BABY.
ARE YOU TIRED? DO YOU WANT ANYTHING?
I'M A LITTLE HUNGRY...
WHAT DO WE DO NOW? THERE'S GOTTA BE SOME WAY TO DROP THESE RIDICULOUS CHARGES.
WOULD I BE ABLE TO FIGHT THEM?
YOU'RE CHARGED WITH A SEGREGATION VIOLATION. FOR BLACK FOLKS IN THE STATE, YOU HAVE NO RIGHTS TO SPEAK OF.
THAT'S WHY YOUR BAIL WAS SO HIGH. IT'S A WAY OF PUNISHING YOU AND KEEPING YOU IN JAIL FOR BREAKING THE LAW.
THEY WOULD HAVE KEPT YOU IN JAIL, TOO, BECAUSE MOST BLACK FOLKS USUALLY DON'T HAVE MONEY.
E.D.? WHAT DO YOU THINK?
I MIGHT HAVE A SOLUTION.
ROSA...WOULD YOU CONSIDER BRINGING A LAWSUIT AGAINST THE BUS COMPANY?

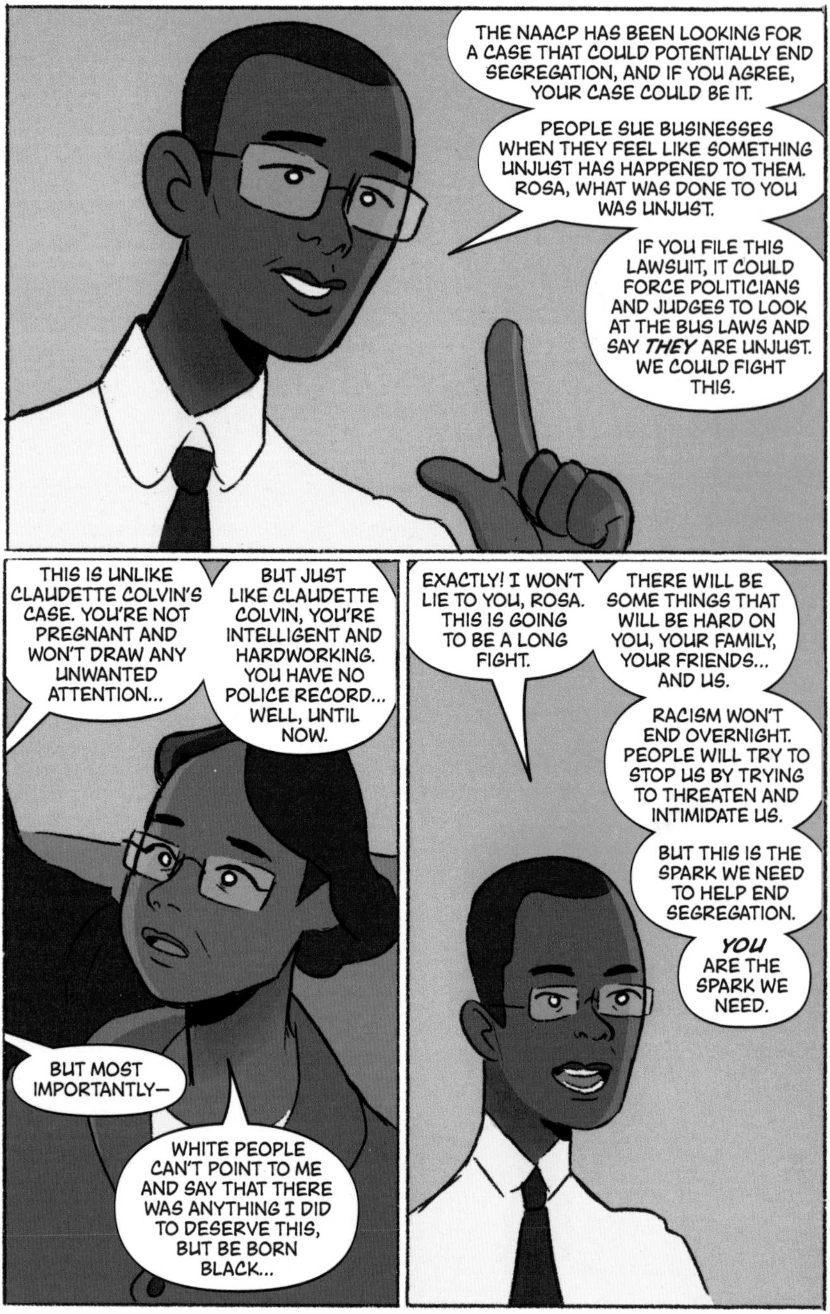
THE NAACP HAS BEEN LOOKING FOR A CASE THAT COULD POTENTIALLY END SEGREGATION, AND IF YOU AGREE, YOUR CASE COULD BE IT.
PEOPLE SUE BUSINESSES WHEN THEY FEEL LIKE SOMETHING UNJUST HAS HAPPENED TO THEM. ROSA, WHAT WAS DONE TO YOU WAS UNJUST.
IF YOU FILE THIS LAWSUIT, IT COULD FORCE POLITICIANS AND JUDGES TO LOOK AT THE BUS LAWS AND SAY *THEY* ARE UNJUST. WE COULD FIGHT THIS.
THIS IS UNLIKE CLAUDETTE COLVIN'S CASE. YOU'RE NOT PREGNANT AND WON'T DRAW ANY UNWANTED ATTENTION...
BUT JUST LIKE CLAUDETTE COLVIN, YOU'RE INTELLIGENT AND HARDWORKING. YOU HAVE NO POLICE RECORD... WELL, UNTIL NOW.
BUT MOST IMPORTANTLY—
WHITE PEOPLE CAN'T POINT TO ME AND SAY THAT THERE WAS ANYTHING I DID TO DESERVE THIS, BUT BE BORN BLACK...
EXACTLY! I WON'T LIE TO YOU, ROSA. THIS IS GOING TO BE A LONG FIGHT.
THERE WILL BE SOME THINGS THAT WILL BE HARD ON YOU, YOUR FAMILY, YOUR FRIENDS... AND US.
RACISM WON'T END OVERNIGHT. PEOPLE WILL TRY TO STOP US BY TRYING TO THREATEN AND INTIMIDATE US.
BUT THIS IS THE SPARK WE NEED TO HELP END SEGREGATION.
YOU ARE THE SPARK WE NEED.

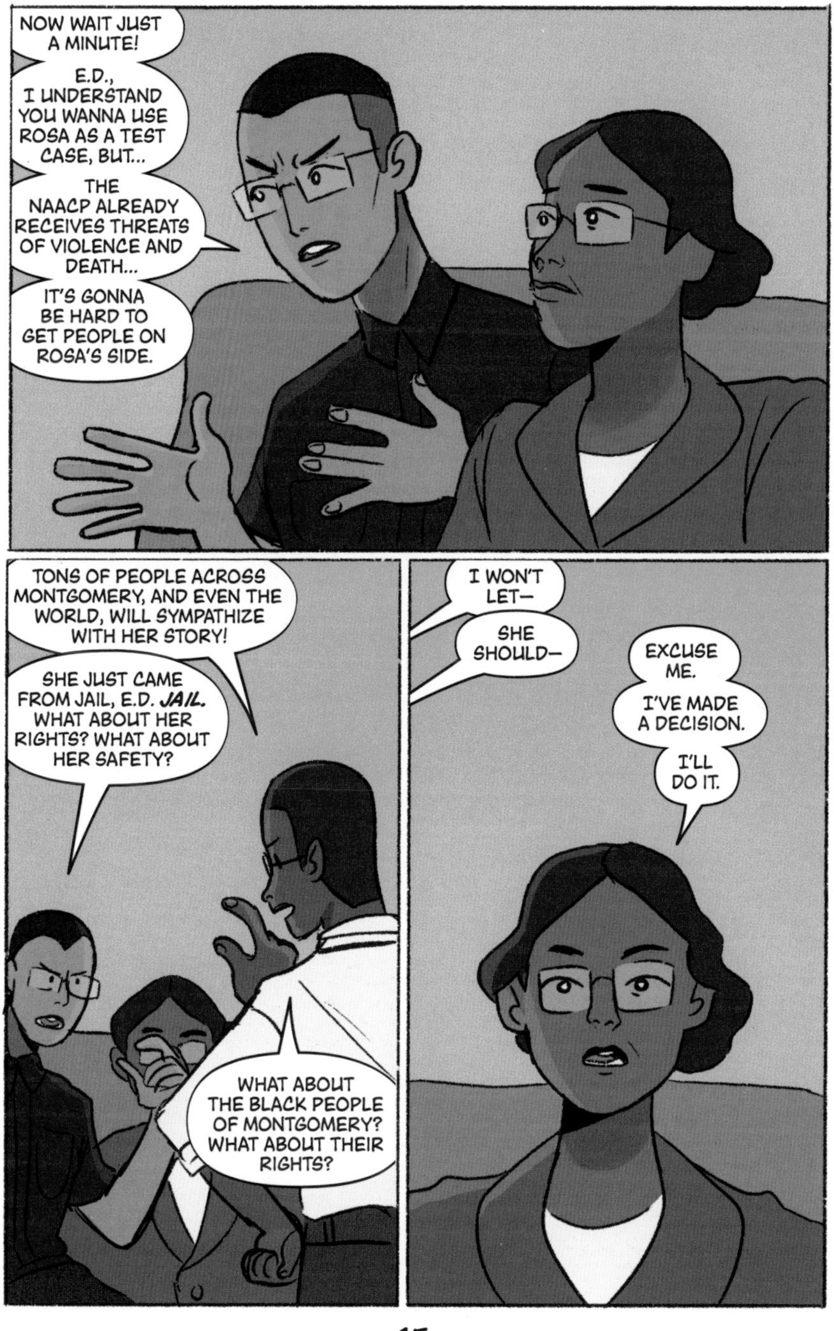
NOW WAIT JUST A MINUTE!
E.D., I UNDERSTAND YOU WANNA USE ROSA AS A TEST CASE, BUT...
THE NAACP ALREADY RECEIVES THREATS OF VIOLENCE AND DEATH...
IT'S GONNA BE HARD TO GET PEOPLE ON ROSA'S SIDE.
TONS OF PEOPLE ACROSS MONTGOMERY, AND EVEN THE WORLD, WILL SYMPATHIZE WITH HER STORY!
SHE JUST CAME FROM JAIL, E.D. *JAIL.* WHAT ABOUT HER RIGHTS? WHAT ABOUT HER SAFETY?
WHAT ABOUT THE BLACK PEOPLE OF MONTGOMERY? WHAT ABOUT THEIR RIGHTS?
I WON'T LET—
SHE SHOULD—
EXCUSE ME.
I'VE MADE A DECISION.
I'LL DO IT.

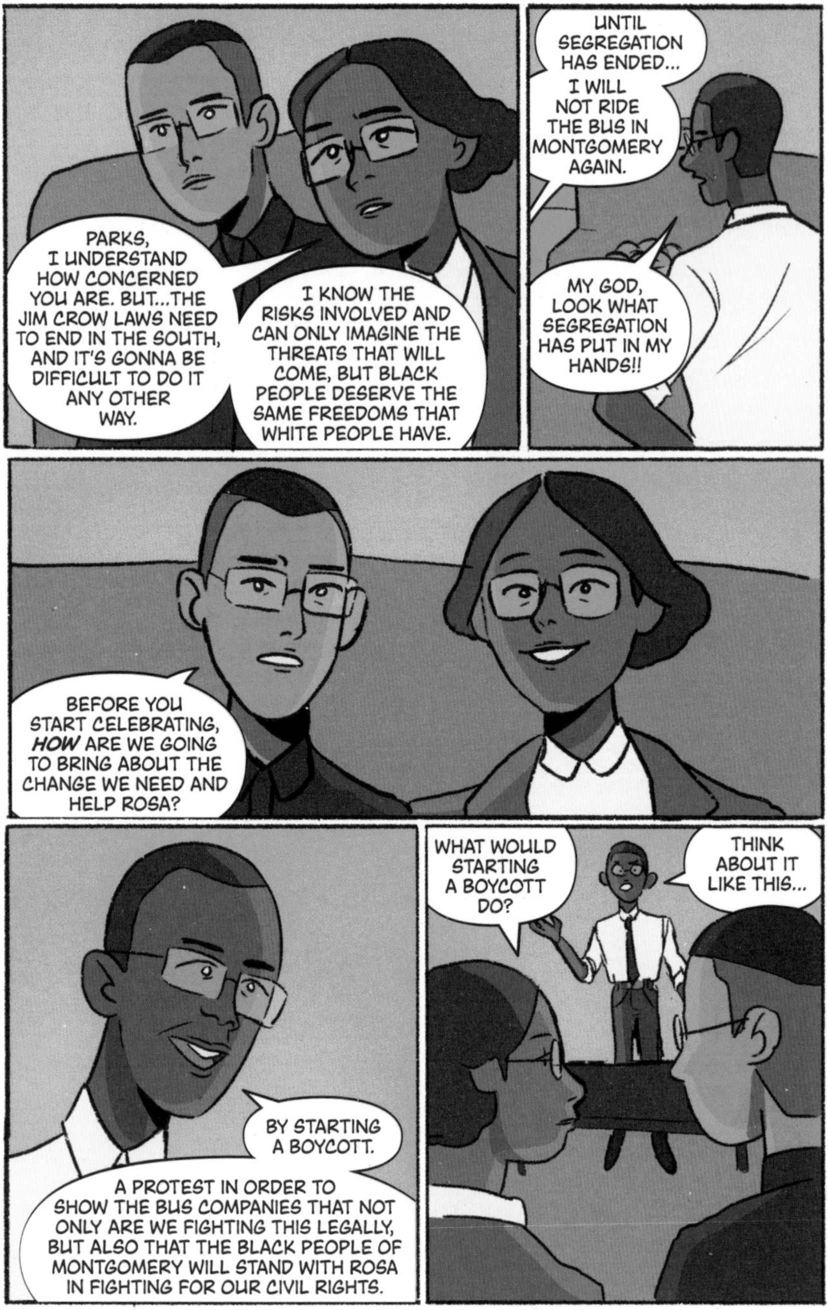
PARKS, I UNDERSTAND HOW CONCERNED YOU ARE. BUT...THE JIM CROW LAWS NEED TO END IN THE SOUTH, AND IT'S GONNA BE DIFFICULT TO DO IT ANY OTHER WAY.
I KNOW THE RISKS INVOLVED AND CAN ONLY IMAGINE THE THREATS THAT WILL COME, BUT BLACK PEOPLE DESERVE THE SAME FREEDOMS THAT WHITE PEOPLE HAVE.
UNTIL SEGREGATION HAS ENDED...
I WILL NOT RIDE THE BUS IN MONTGOMERY AGAIN.
MY GOD, LOOK WHAT SEGREGATION HAS PUT IN MY HANDS!!
BEFORE YOU START CELEBRATING, *HOW* ARE WE GOING TO BRING ABOUT THE CHANGE WE NEED AND HELP ROSA?
BY STARTING A BOYCOTT.
A PROTEST IN ORDER TO SHOW THE BUS COMPANIES THAT NOT ONLY ARE WE FIGHTING THIS LEGALLY, BUT ALSO THAT THE BLACK PEOPLE OF MONTGOMERY WILL STAND WITH ROSA IN FIGHTING FOR OUR CIVIL RIGHTS.
WHAT WOULD STARTING A BOYCOTT DO?
THINK ABOUT IT LIKE THIS...

Jim Crow Laws

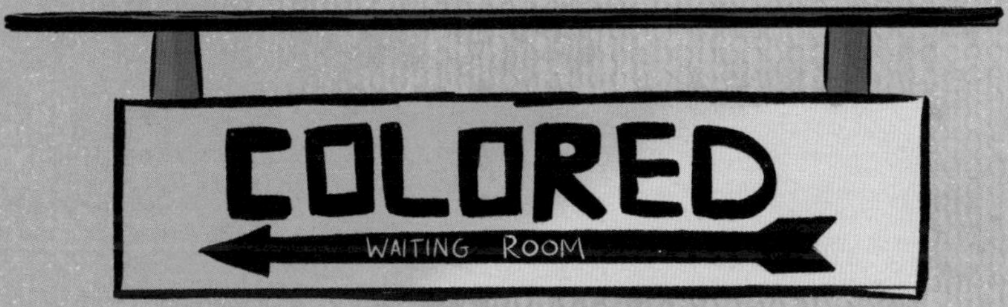
COLORED
WAITING ROOM

After the Thirteenth Amendment to the US Constitution was signed into law in December of 1865, states in the American South quickly created laws that made it legal to separate people by race. They were known as Jim Crow laws. These laws prohibited Black people from going to the same restaurants, attending the same schools, or even sitting in the same sections of the bus. Jim Crow laws also made voting harder for Black people by enforcing hard literacy tests and an expensive voting tax (called a poll tax), which most people couldn't afford.

In 1954, the Supreme Court case of *Brown v. Board of Education* declared Jim Crow laws unconstitutional. Ten years later, Jim Crow laws were made illegal by the Civil Rights Act of 1964 and the Voting Rights Act of 1965.

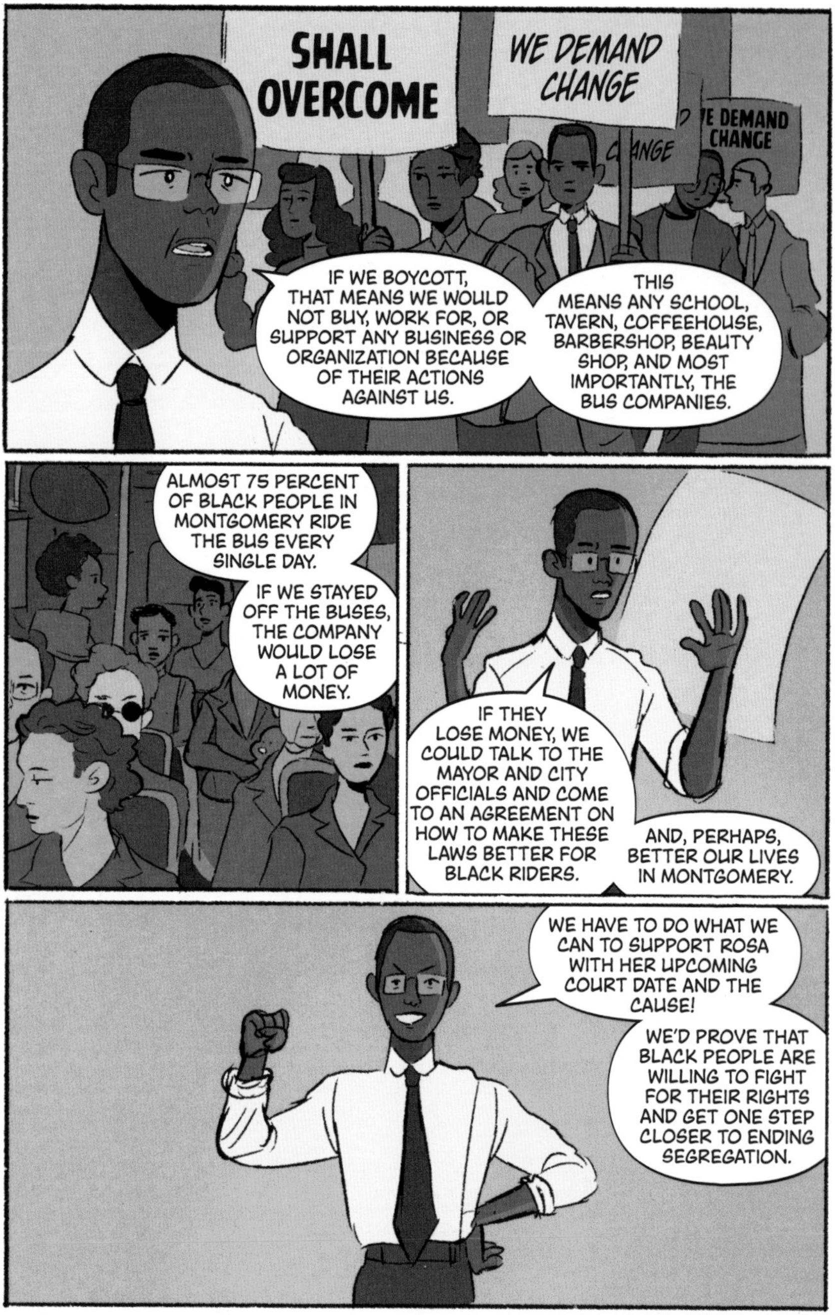
SHALL OVERCOME
WE DEMAND CHANGE
IF WE BOYCOTT, THAT MEANS WE WOULD NOT BUY, WORK FOR, OR SUPPORT ANY BUSINESS OR ORGANIZATION BECAUSE OF THEIR ACTIONS AGAINST US.
THIS MEANS ANY SCHOOL, TAVERN, COFFEEHOUSE, BARBERSHOP, BEAUTY SHOP, AND MOST IMPORTANTLY, THE BUS COMPANIES.
ALMOST 75 PERCENT OF BLACK PEOPLE IN MONTGOMERY RIDE THE BUS EVERY SINGLE DAY.
IF WE STAYED OFF THE BUSES, THE COMPANY WOULD LOSE A LOT OF MONEY.
IF THEY LOSE MONEY, WE COULD TALK TO THE MAYOR AND CITY OFFICIALS AND COME TO AN AGREEMENT ON HOW TO MAKE THESE LAWS BETTER FOR BLACK RIDERS.
AND, PERHAPS, BETTER OUR LIVES IN MONTGOMERY.
WE HAVE TO DO WHAT WE CAN TO SUPPORT ROSA WITH HER UPCOMING COURT DATE AND THE CAUSE!
WE'D PROVE THAT BLACK PEOPLE ARE WILLING TO FIGHT FOR THEIR RIGHTS AND GET ONE STEP CLOSER TO ENDING SEGREGATION.

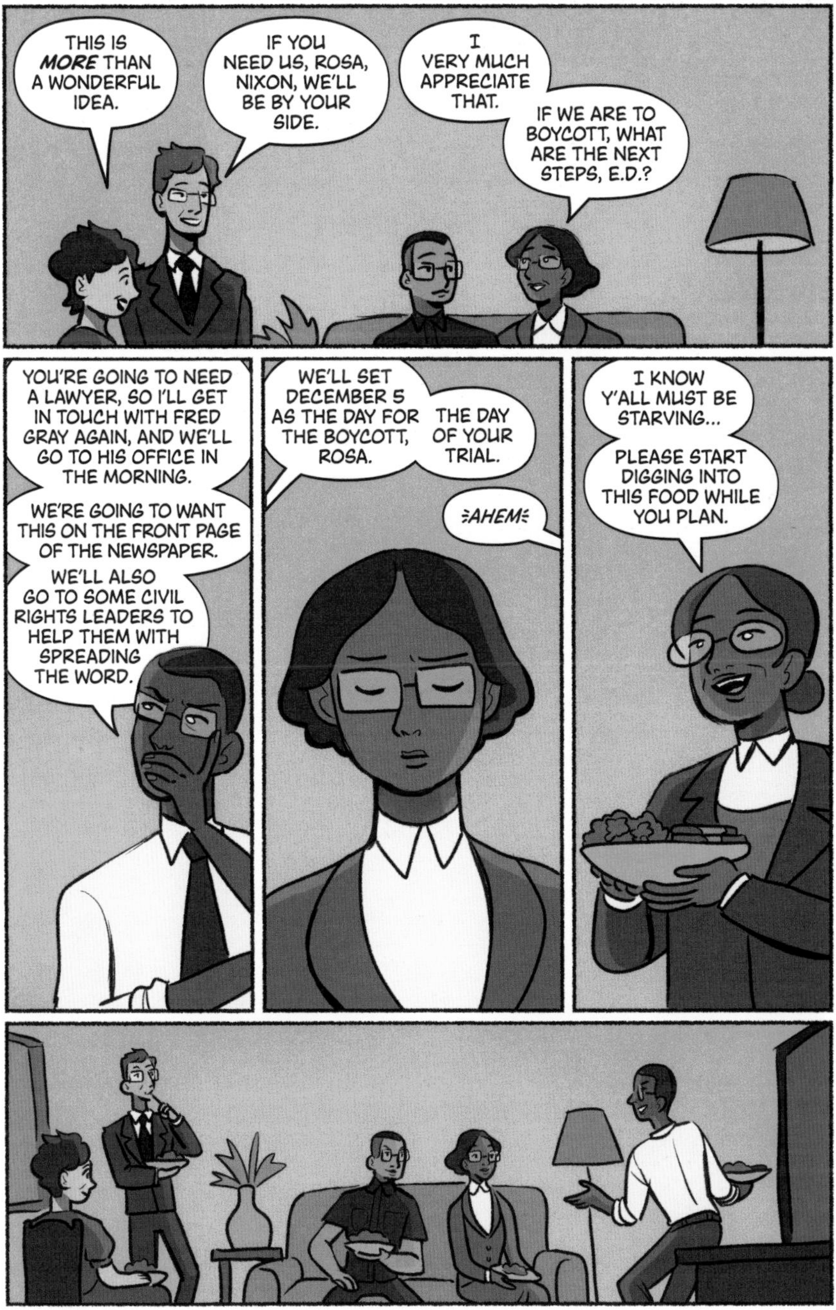
THIS IS *MORE* THAN A WONDERFUL IDEA.
IF YOU NEED US, ROSA, NIXON, WE'LL BE BY YOUR SIDE.
I VERY MUCH APPRECIATE THAT.
IF WE ARE TO BOYCOTT, WHAT ARE THE NEXT STEPS, E.D.?
YOU'RE GOING TO NEED A LAWYER, SO I'LL GET IN TOUCH WITH FRED GRAY AGAIN, AND WE'LL GO TO HIS OFFICE IN THE MORNING.
WE'RE GOING TO WANT THIS ON THE FRONT PAGE OF THE NEWSPAPER.
WE'LL ALSO GO TO SOME CIVIL RIGHTS LEADERS TO HELP THEM WITH SPREADING THE WORD.
WE'LL SET DECEMBER 5 AS THE DAY FOR THE BOYCOTT, ROSA.
THE DAY OF YOUR TRIAL.
AHEM
I KNOW Y'ALL MUST BE STARVING...
PLEASE START DIGGING INTO THIS FOOD WHILE YOU PLAN.

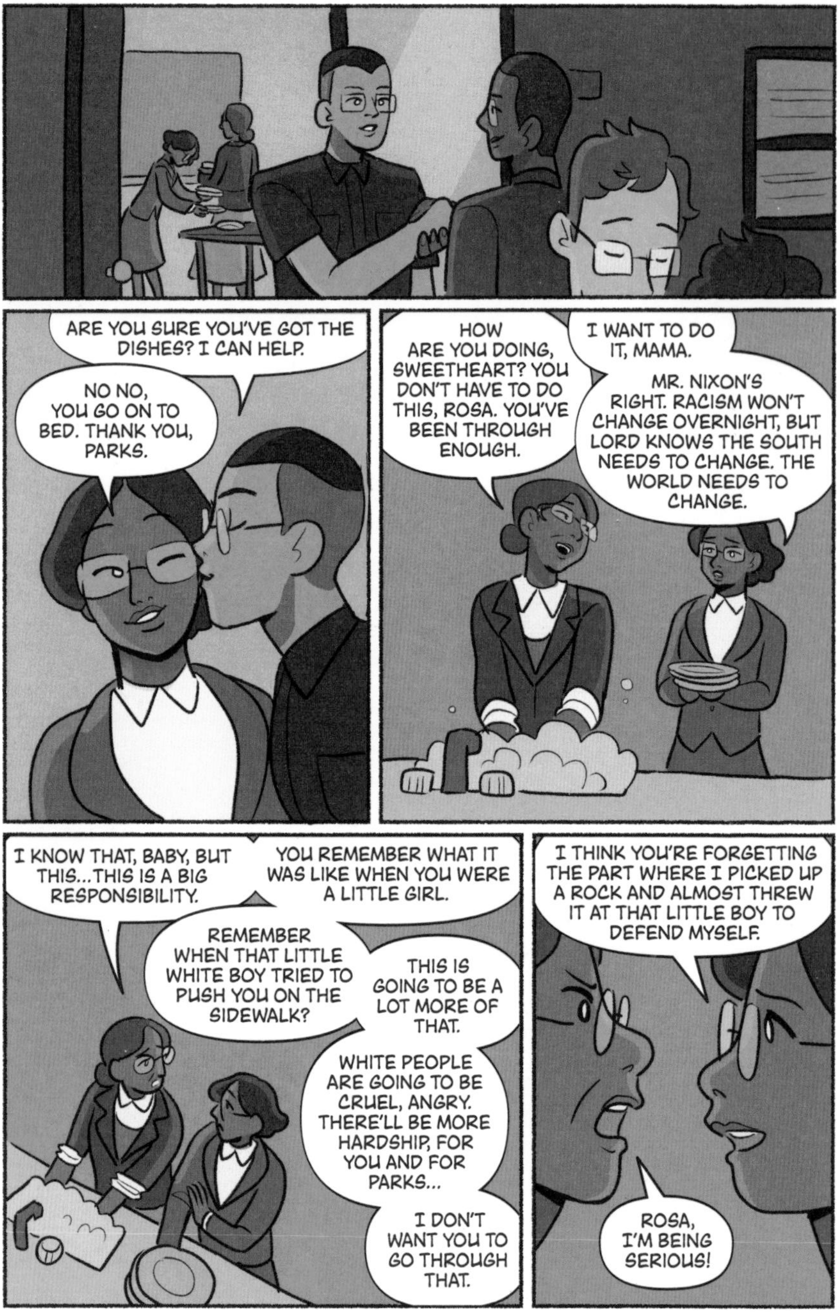
ARE YOU SURE YOU'VE GOT THE DISHES? I CAN HELP.
NO NO, YOU GO ON TO BED. THANK YOU, PARKS.
HOW ARE YOU DOING, SWEETHEART? YOU DON'T HAVE TO DO THIS, ROSA. YOU'VE BEEN THROUGH ENOUGH.
I WANT TO DO IT, MAMA.
MR. NIXON'S RIGHT. RACISM WON'T CHANGE OVERNIGHT, BUT LORD KNOWS THE SOUTH NEEDS TO CHANGE. THE WORLD NEEDS TO CHANGE.
I KNOW THAT, BABY, BUT THIS...THIS IS A BIG RESPONSIBILITY.
YOU REMEMBER WHAT IT WAS LIKE WHEN YOU WERE A LITTLE GIRL.
REMEMBER WHEN THAT LITTLE WHITE BOY TRIED TO PUSH YOU ON THE SIDEWALK?
THIS IS GOING TO BE A LOT MORE OF THAT.
WHITE PEOPLE ARE GOING TO BE CRUEL, ANGRY. THERE'LL BE MORE HARDSHIP, FOR YOU AND FOR PARKS...
I DON'T WANT YOU TO GO THROUGH THAT.
I THINK YOU'RE FORGETTING THE PART WHERE I PICKED UP A ROCK AND ALMOST THREW IT AT THAT LITTLE BOY TO DEFEND MYSELF.
ROSA, I'M BEING SERIOUS!

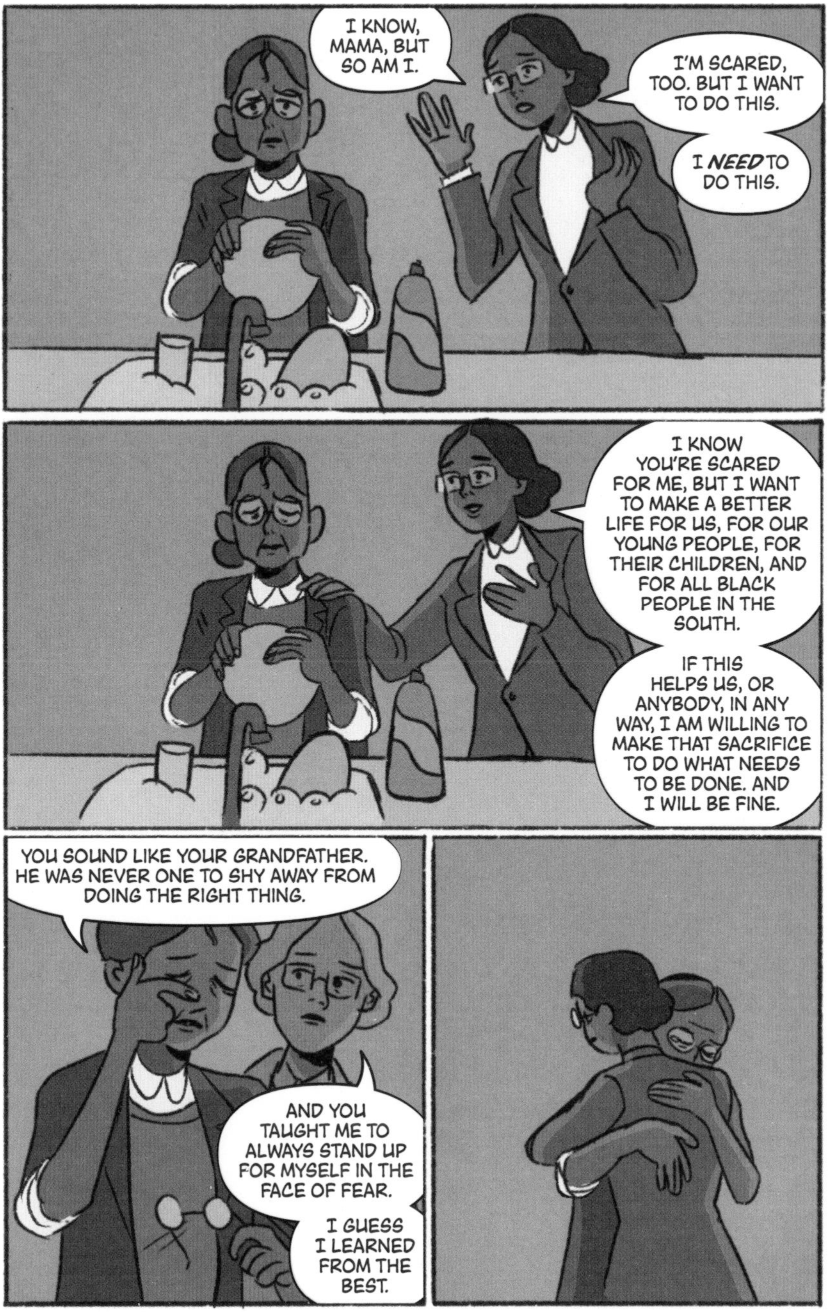
I KNOW, MAMA, BUT SO AM I.
I'M SCARED, TOO. BUT I WANT TO DO THIS.
I *NEED* TO DO THIS.
I KNOW YOU'RE SCARED FOR ME, BUT I WANT TO MAKE A BETTER LIFE FOR US, FOR OUR YOUNG PEOPLE, FOR THEIR CHILDREN, AND FOR ALL BLACK PEOPLE IN THE SOUTH.
IF THIS HELPS US, OR ANYBODY, IN ANY WAY, I AM WILLING TO MAKE THAT SACRIFICE TO DO WHAT NEEDS TO BE DONE. AND I WILL BE FINE.
YOU SOUND LIKE YOUR GRANDFATHER. HE WAS NEVER ONE TO SHY AWAY FROM DOING THE RIGHT THING.
AND YOU TAUGHT ME TO ALWAYS STAND UP FOR MYSELF IN THE FACE OF FEAR.
I GUESS I LEARNED FROM THE BEST.

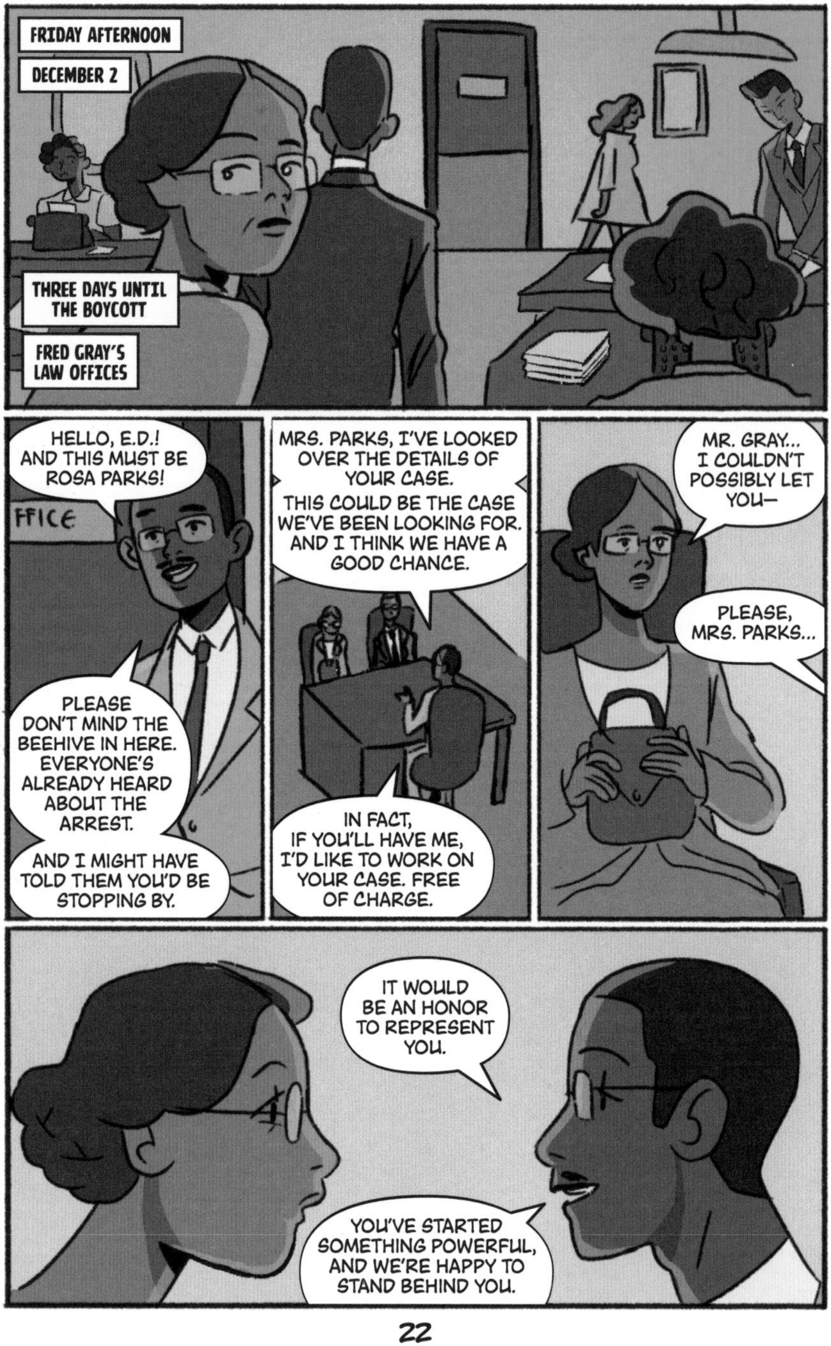
FRIDAY AFTERNOON
DECEMBER 2
THREE DAYS UNTIL THE BOYCOTT
FRED GRAY'S LAW OFFICES
HELLO, E.D.! AND THIS MUST BE ROSA PARKS!
FFICE
PLEASE DON'T MIND THE BEEHIVE IN HERE. EVERYONE'S ALREADY HEARD ABOUT THE ARREST.
AND I MIGHT HAVE TOLD THEM YOU'D BE STOPPING BY.
MRS. PARKS, I'VE LOOKED OVER THE DETAILS OF YOUR CASE.
THIS COULD BE THE CASE WE'VE BEEN LOOKING FOR. AND I THINK WE HAVE A GOOD CHANCE.
IN FACT, IF YOU'LL HAVE ME, I'D LIKE TO WORK ON YOUR CASE. FREE OF CHARGE.
MR. GRAY... I COULDN'T POSSIBLY LET YOU—
PLEASE, MRS. PARKS...
IT WOULD BE AN HONOR TO REPRESENT YOU.
YOU'VE STARTED SOMETHING POWERFUL, AND WE'RE HAPPY TO STAND BEHIND YOU.

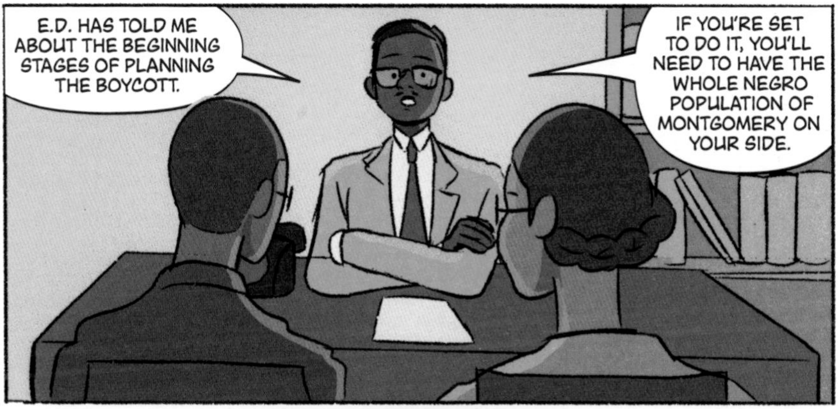
E.D. HAS TOLD ME ABOUT THE BEGINNING STAGES OF PLANNING THE BOYCOTT.
IF YOU'RE SET TO DO IT, YOU'LL NEED TO HAVE THE WHOLE NEGRO POPULATION OF MONTGOMERY ON YOUR SIDE.

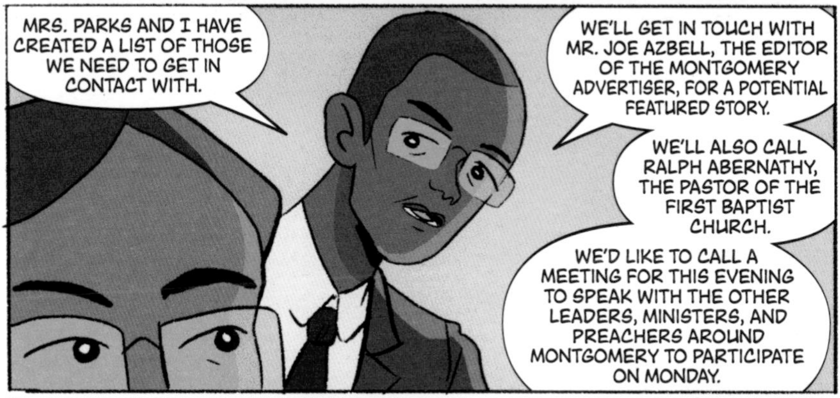
MRS. PARKS AND I HAVE CREATED A LIST OF THOSE WE NEED TO GET IN CONTACT WITH.
WE'LL GET IN TOUCH WITH MR. JOE AZBELL, THE EDITOR OF THE MONTGOMERY ADVERTISER, FOR A POTENTIAL FEATURED STORY.
WE'LL ALSO CALL RALPH ABERNATHY, THE PASTOR OF THE FIRST BAPTIST CHURCH.
WE'D LIKE TO CALL A MEETING FOR THIS EVENING TO SPEAK WITH THE OTHER LEADERS, MINISTERS, AND PREACHERS AROUND MONTGOMERY TO PARTICIPATE ON MONDAY.

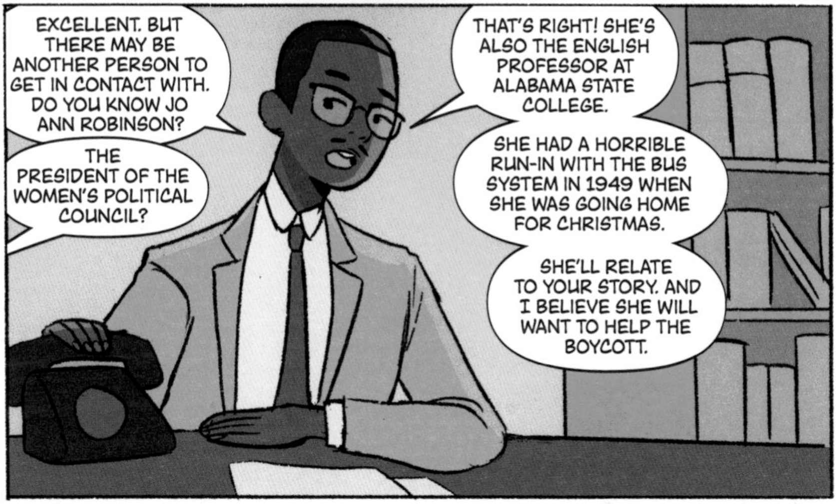
EXCELLENT. BUT THERE MAY BE ANOTHER PERSON TO GET IN CONTACT WITH. DO YOU KNOW JO ANN ROBINSON?
THE PRESIDENT OF THE WOMEN'S POLITICAL COUNCIL?
THAT'S RIGHT! SHE'S ALSO THE ENGLISH PROFESSOR AT ALABAMA STATE COLLEGE.
SHE HAD A HORRIBLE RUN-IN WITH THE BUS SYSTEM IN 1949 WHEN SHE WAS GOING HOME FOR CHRISTMAS.
SHE'LL RELATE TO YOUR STORY. AND I BELIEVE SHE WILL WANT TO HELP THE BOYCOTT.

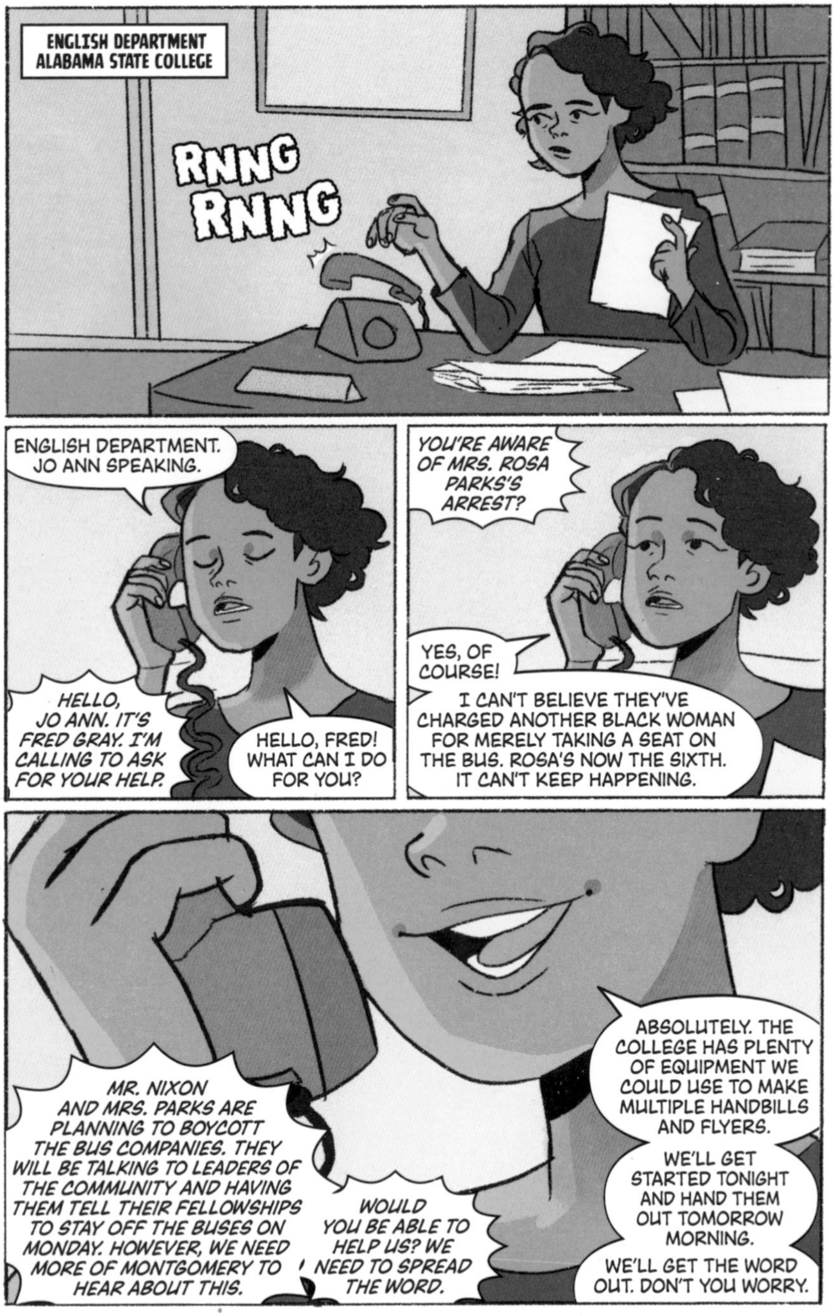

ENGLISH DEPARTMENT
ALABAMA STATE COLLEGE
RNNG
RNNG
ENGLISH DEPARTMENT. JO ANN SPEAKING.
HELLO, JO ANN. IT'S FRED GRAY. I'M CALLING TO ASK FOR YOUR HELP.
HELLO, FRED! WHAT CAN I DO FOR YOU?
YOU'RE AWARE OF MRS. ROSA PARKS'S ARREST?
YES, OF COURSE!
I CAN'T BELIEVE THEY'VE CHARGED ANOTHER BLACK WOMAN FOR MERELY TAKING A SEAT ON THE BUS. ROSA'S NOW THE SIXTH. IT CAN'T KEEP HAPPENING.
MR. NIXON AND MRS. PARKS ARE PLANNING TO BOYCOTT THE BUS COMPANIES. THEY WILL BE TALKING TO LEADERS OF THE COMMUNITY AND HAVING THEM TELL THEIR FELLOWSHIPS TO STAY OFF THE BUSES ON MONDAY. HOWEVER, WE NEED MORE OF MONTGOMERY TO HEAR ABOUT THIS.
WOULD YOU BE ABLE TO HELP US? WE NEED TO SPREAD THE WORD.
ABSOLUTELY. THE COLLEGE HAS PLENTY OF EQUIPMENT WE COULD USE TO MAKE MULTIPLE HANDBILLS AND FLYERS.
WE'LL GET STARTED TONIGHT AND HAND THEM OUT TOMORROW MORNING.
WE'LL GET THE WORD OUT. DON'T YOU WORRY.

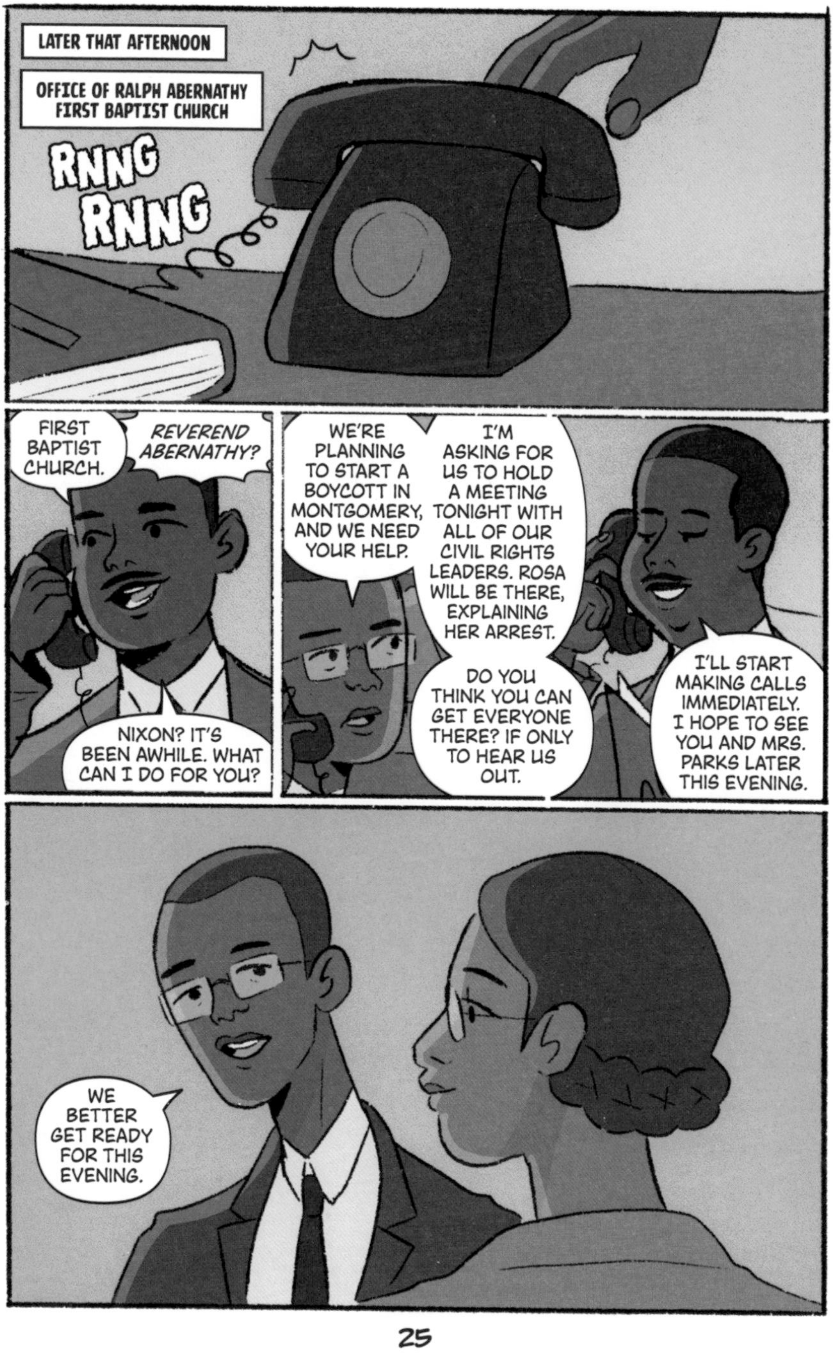
LATER THAT AFTERNOON
OFFICE OF RALPH ABERNATHY FIRST BAPTIST CHURCH
RNNG RNNG
FIRST BAPTIST CHURCH.
REVEREND ABERNATHY?
NIXON? IT'S BEEN AWHILE. WHAT CAN I DO FOR YOU?
WE'RE PLANNING TO START A BOYCOTT IN MONTGOMERY, AND WE NEED YOUR HELP.
I'M ASKING FOR US TO HOLD A MEETING TONIGHT WITH ALL OF OUR CIVIL RIGHTS LEADERS. ROSA WILL BE THERE, EXPLAINING HER ARREST.
DO YOU THINK YOU CAN GET EVERYONE THERE? IF ONLY TO HEAR US OUT.
I'LL START MAKING CALLS IMMEDIATELY. I HOPE TO SEE YOU AND MRS. PARKS LATER THIS EVENING.
WE BETTER GET READY FOR THIS EVENING.

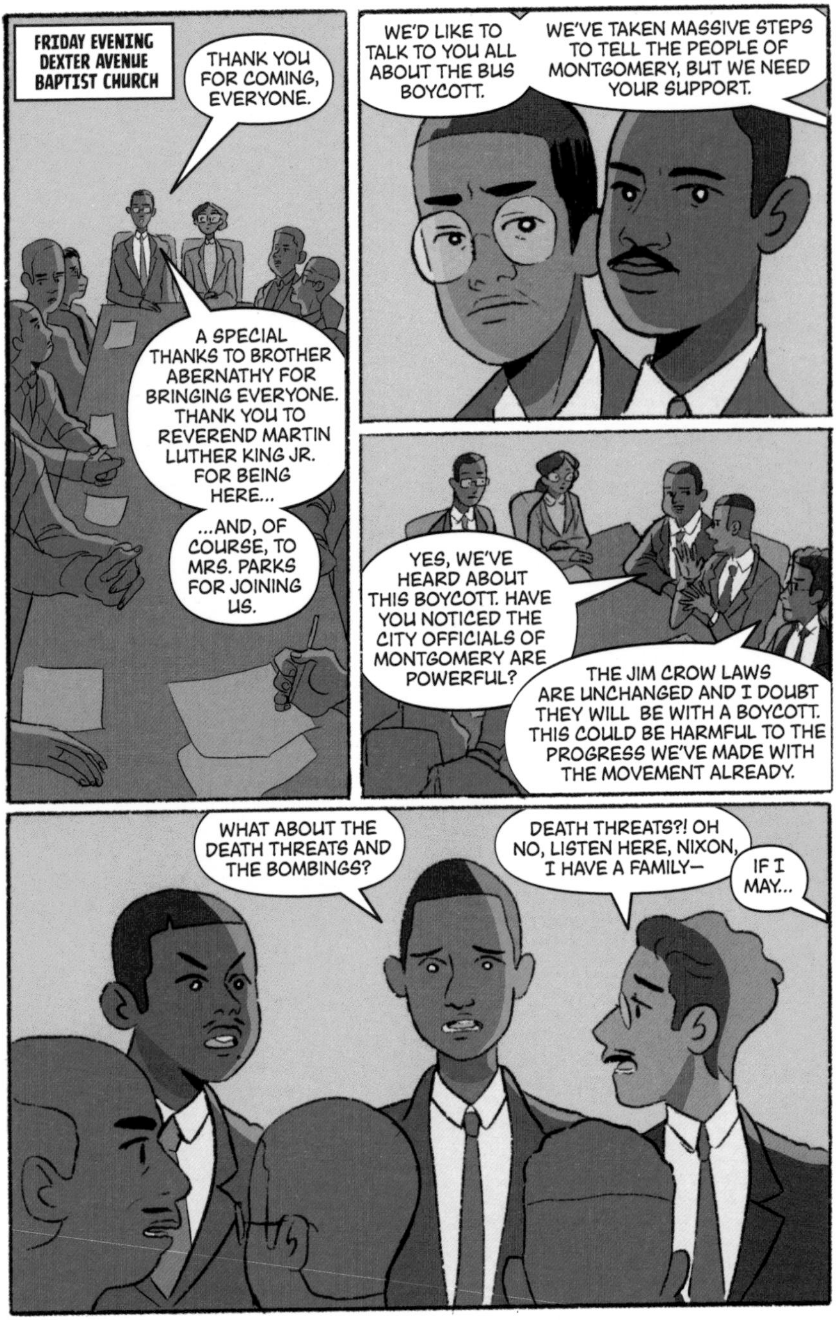
FRIDAY EVENING DEXTER AVENUE BAPTIST CHURCH
THANK YOU FOR COMING, EVERYONE.
A SPECIAL THANKS TO BROTHER ABERNATHY FOR BRINGING EVERYONE. THANK YOU TO REVEREND MARTIN LUTHER KING JR. FOR BEING HERE...
...AND, OF COURSE, TO MRS. PARKS FOR JOINING US.
WE'D LIKE TO TALK TO YOU ALL ABOUT THE BUS BOYCOTT.
WE'VE TAKEN MASSIVE STEPS TO TELL THE PEOPLE OF MONTGOMERY, BUT WE NEED YOUR SUPPORT.
YES, WE'VE HEARD ABOUT THIS BOYCOTT. HAVE YOU NOTICED THE CITY OFFICIALS OF MONTGOMERY ARE POWERFUL?
THE JIM CROW LAWS ARE UNCHANGED AND I DOUBT THEY WILL BE WITH A BOYCOTT. THIS COULD BE HARMFUL TO THE PROGRESS WE'VE MADE WITH THE MOVEMENT ALREADY.
WHAT ABOUT THE DEATH THREATS AND THE BOMBINGS?
DEATH THREATS?! OH NO, LISTEN HERE, NIXON, I HAVE A FAMILY—
IF I MAY...

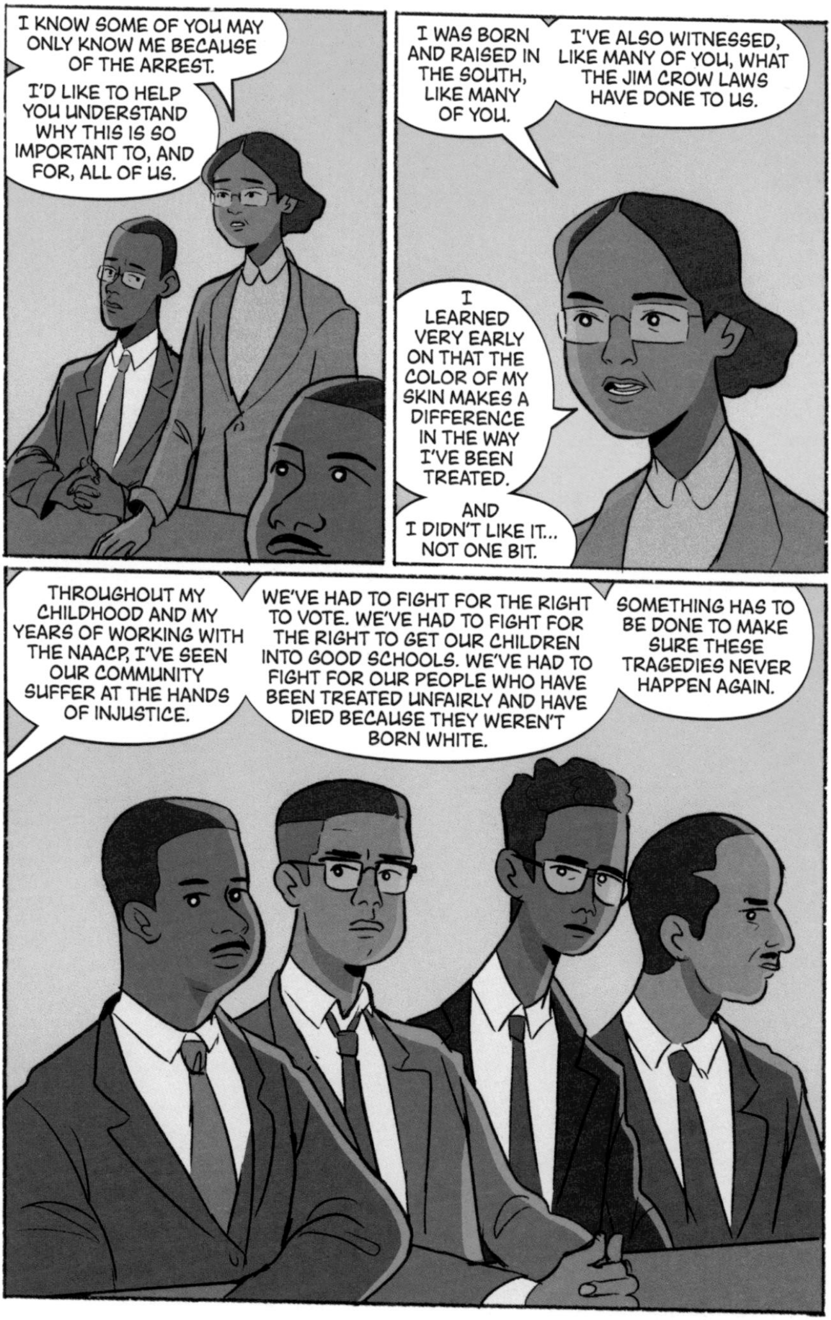
I KNOW SOME OF YOU MAY ONLY KNOW ME BECAUSE OF THE ARREST.
I'D LIKE TO HELP YOU UNDERSTAND WHY THIS IS SO IMPORTANT TO, AND FOR, ALL OF US.
I WAS BORN AND RAISED IN THE SOUTH, LIKE MANY OF YOU.
I'VE ALSO WITNESSED, LIKE MANY OF YOU, WHAT THE JIM CROW LAWS HAVE DONE TO US.
I LEARNED VERY EARLY ON THAT THE COLOR OF MY SKIN MAKES A DIFFERENCE IN THE WAY I'VE BEEN TREATED.
AND I DIDN'T LIKE IT... NOT ONE BIT.
THROUGHOUT MY CHILDHOOD AND MY YEARS OF WORKING WITH THE NAACP, I'VE SEEN OUR COMMUNITY SUFFER AT THE HANDS OF INJUSTICE.
WE'VE HAD TO FIGHT FOR THE RIGHT TO VOTE. WE'VE HAD TO FIGHT FOR THE RIGHT TO GET OUR CHILDREN INTO GOOD SCHOOLS. WE'VE HAD TO FIGHT FOR OUR PEOPLE WHO HAVE BEEN TREATED UNFAIRLY AND HAVE DIED BECAUSE THEY WEREN'T BORN WHITE.
SOMETHING HAS TO BE DONE TO MAKE SURE THESE TRAGEDIES NEVER HAPPEN AGAIN.

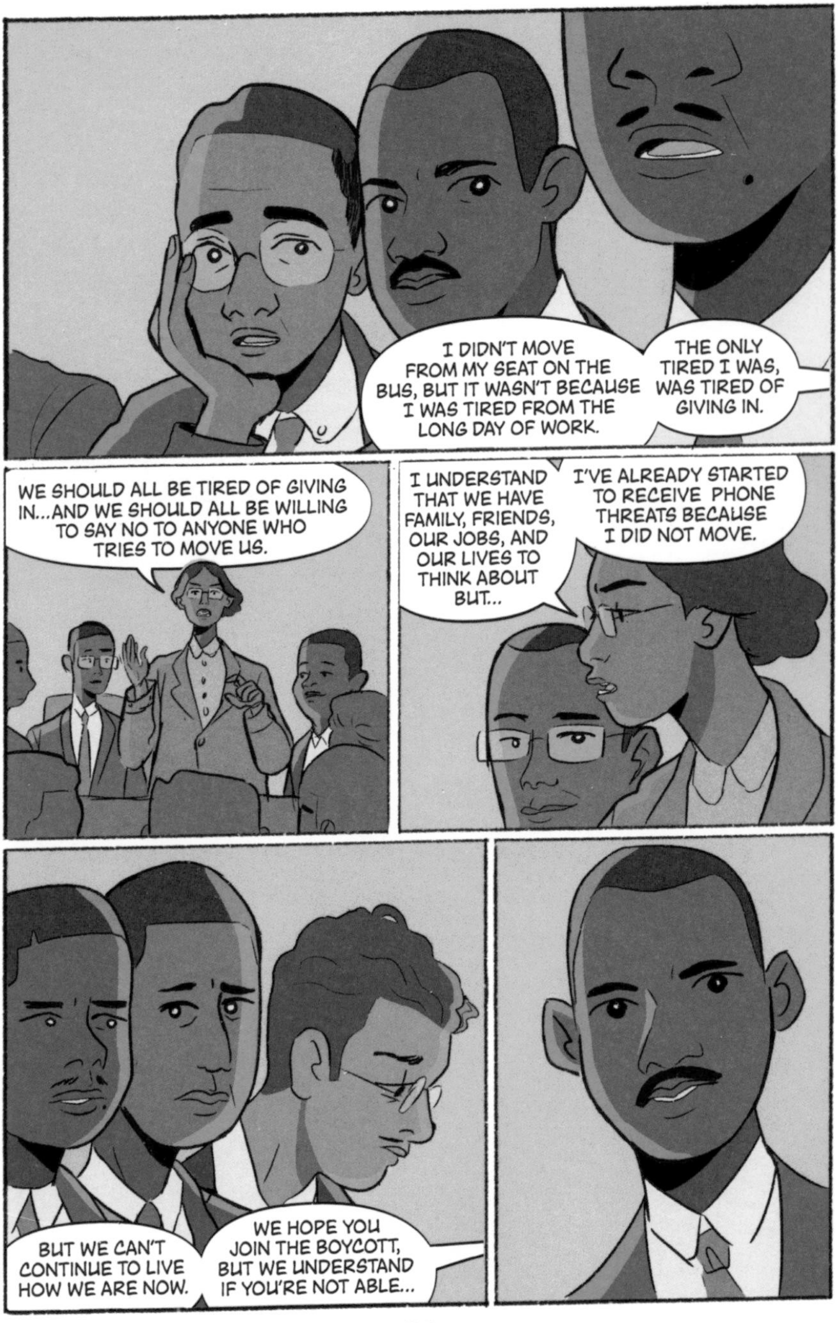
I DIDN'T MOVE FROM MY SEAT ON THE BUS, BUT IT WASN'T BECAUSE I WAS TIRED FROM THE LONG DAY OF WORK.
THE ONLY TIRED I WAS, WAS TIRED OF GIVING IN.
WE SHOULD ALL BE TIRED OF GIVING IN...AND WE SHOULD ALL BE WILLING TO SAY NO TO ANYONE WHO TRIES TO MOVE US.
I UNDERSTAND THAT WE HAVE FAMILY, FRIENDS, OUR JOBS, AND OUR LIVES TO THINK ABOUT BUT...
I'VE ALREADY STARTED TO RECEIVE PHONE THREATS BECAUSE I DID NOT MOVE.
BUT WE CAN'T CONTINUE TO LIVE HOW WE ARE NOW.
WE HOPE YOU JOIN THE BOYCOTT, BUT WE UNDERSTAND IF YOU'RE NOT ABLE...

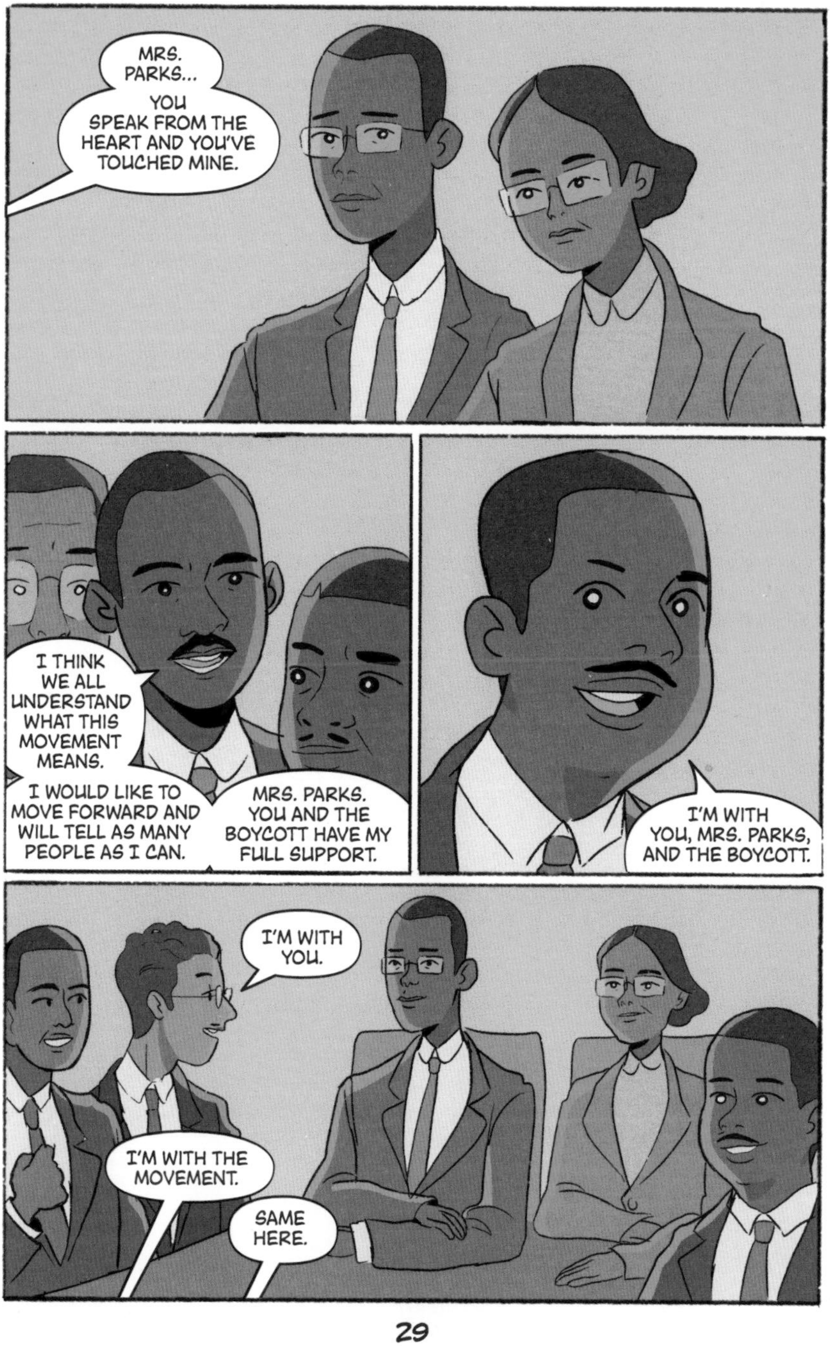
MRS. PARKS...
YOU SPEAK FROM THE HEART AND YOU'VE TOUCHED MINE.
I THINK WE ALL UNDERSTAND WHAT THIS MOVEMENT MEANS.
I WOULD LIKE TO MOVE FORWARD AND WILL TELL AS MANY PEOPLE AS I CAN.
MRS. PARKS. YOU AND THE BOYCOTT HAVE MY FULL SUPPORT.
I'M WITH YOU, MRS. PARKS, AND THE BOYCOTT.
I'M WITH YOU.
I'M WITH THE MOVEMENT.
SAME HERE.

Martin Luther King Jr.

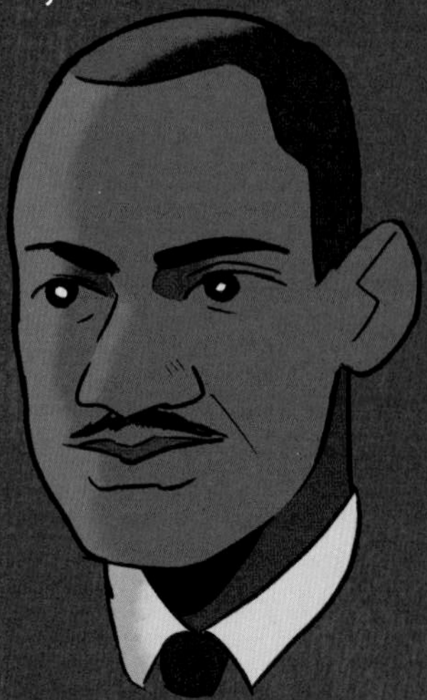

Born in Atlanta, Georgia, on January 15, 1929, Martin Luther King Jr. was a minister and civil rights activist. Martin was born into a religious family who gave him the Christian values he would come to display when it came to his activism. He encouraged his fellow activists to practice nonviolent protests.

Martin Luther King Jr. became a force for African American rights in the South, starting with the Montgomery Bus Boycott. From there, he was the president of the Southern Christian Leadership Conference, which allowed him to participate actively in planning many nonviolent protests. The largest and most famous was the March on Washington (1963) to achieve both civil and economic rights for African Americans. There, King would deliver his most famous speech, "I Have a Dream," to over 200,000 people.

Martin Luther King Jr. was a pivotal person in the civil rights movement. His words and actions helped inspire many people to fight for civil liberties. Tragically, Martin Luther King Jr. was shot to death in Memphis, Tennessee, on April 4, 1968.

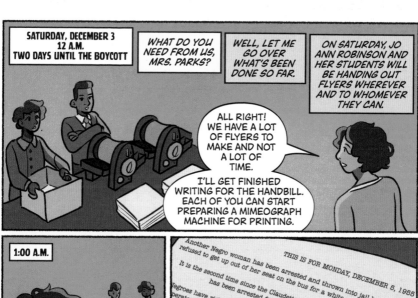

SATURDAY, DECEMBER 3
12 A.M.
TWO DAYS UNTIL THE BOYCOTT

WHAT DO YOU NEED FROM US, MRS. PARKS?

WELL, LET ME GO OVER WHAT'S BEEN DONE SO FAR.

ON SATURDAY, JO ANN ROBINSON AND HER STUDENTS WILL BE HANDING OUT FLYERS WHEREVER AND TO WHOMEVER THEY CAN.

ALL RIGHT! WE HAVE A LOT OF FLYERS TO MAKE AND NOT A LOT OF TIME.

I'LL GET FINISHED WRITING FOR THE HANDBILL. EACH OF YOU CAN START PREPARING A MIMEOGRAPH MACHINE FOR PRINTING.

1:00 A.M.

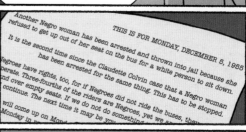

THIS IS FOR MONDAY, DECEMBER 5, 1955

Another Negro woman has been arrested and thrown into jail because she refused to get up out of her seat on the bus for a white person to sit down.

It is the second time since the Claudette Colvin case that a Negro woman has been arrested for the same thing. This has to be stopped.

Negroes have rights, too, for if Negroes did not ride the buses, they could not operate. Three-fourths of the riders are Negroes, yet we are arrested, or have to stand over empty seats. If we do not do something to stop these arrests, they will continue. The next time it may be you, or your daughter, or mother.

This woman's case will come up on Monday...

Monday in...

2:00 A.M.

3:00 A.M.

THAT'S THE LAST OF 'EM.

WHAT SHOULD WE DO NOW?

WE NOW HAND OUT OVER 50,000 HANDBILLS TO WHOMEVER WE CAN THROUGHOUT THE WEEKEND, AND PRAY PEOPLE STAY OFF THOSE BUSES.

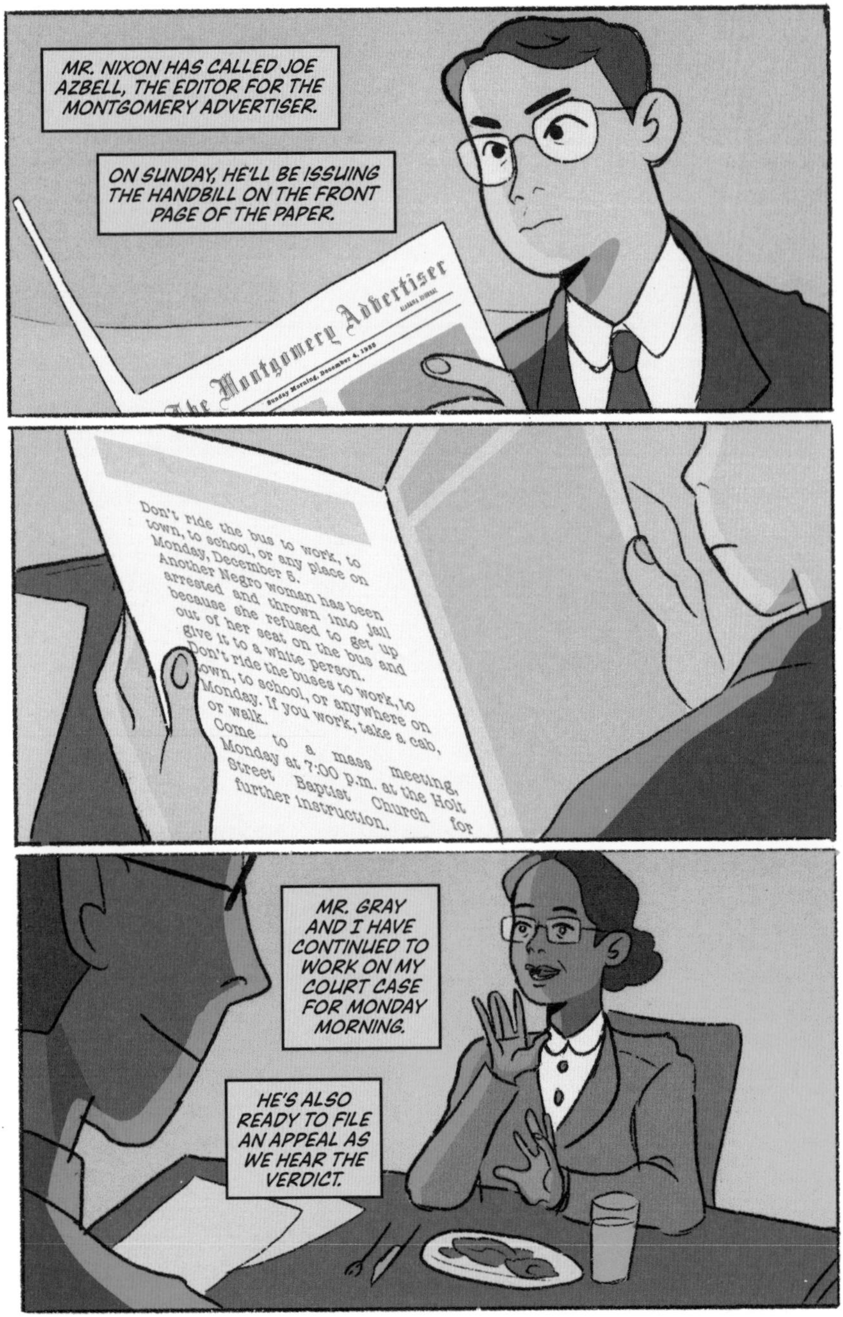
MR. NIXON HAS CALLED JOE AZBELL, THE EDITOR FOR THE MONTGOMERY ADVERTISER.
ON SUNDAY, HE'LL BE ISSUING THE HANDBILL ON THE FRONT PAGE OF THE PAPER.
The Montgomery Advertiser
Don't ride the bus to work, to town, to school, or any place on Monday, December 5.
Another Negro woman has been arrested and thrown into jail because she refused to get up out of her seat on the bus and give it to a white person.
Don't ride the buses to work, to town, to school, or anywhere on Monday. If you work, take a cab, or walk.
Come to a mass meeting, Monday at 7:00 p.m. at the Holt Street Baptist Church for further instruction.
MR. GRAY AND I HAVE CONTINUED TO WORK ON MY COURT CASE FOR MONDAY MORNING.
HE'S ALSO READY TO FILE AN APPEAL AS WE HEAR THE VERDICT.

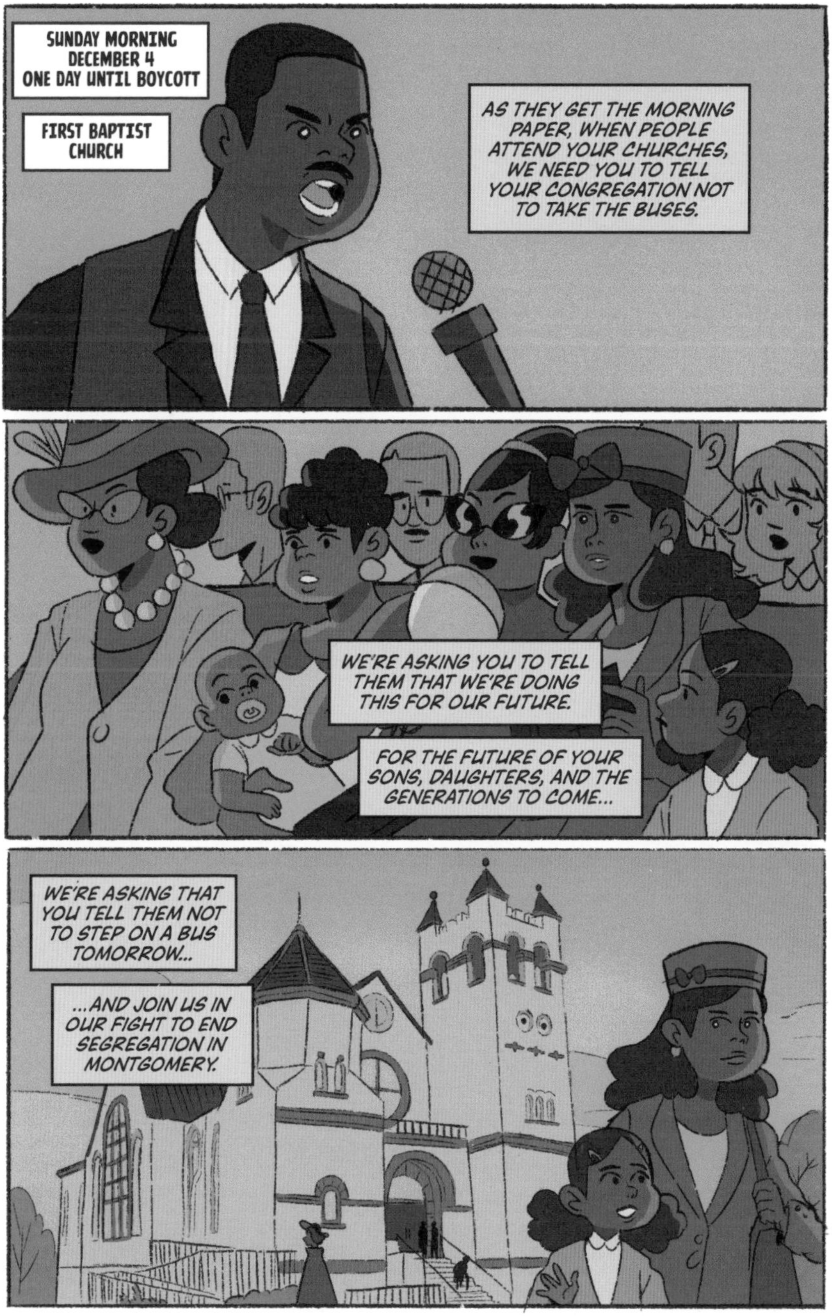
SUNDAY MORNING
DECEMBER 4
ONE DAY UNTIL BOYCOTT
FIRST BAPTIST CHURCH
AS THEY GET THE MORNING PAPER, WHEN PEOPLE ATTEND YOUR CHURCHES, WE NEED YOU TO TELL YOUR CONGREGATION NOT TO TAKE THE BUSES.
WE'RE ASKING YOU TO TELL THEM THAT WE'RE DOING THIS FOR OUR FUTURE.
FOR THE FUTURE OF YOUR SONS, DAUGHTERS, AND THE GENERATIONS TO COME...
WE'RE ASKING THAT YOU TELL THEM NOT TO STEP ON A BUS TOMORROW...
...AND JOIN US IN OUR FIGHT TO END SEGREGATION IN MONTGOMERY.

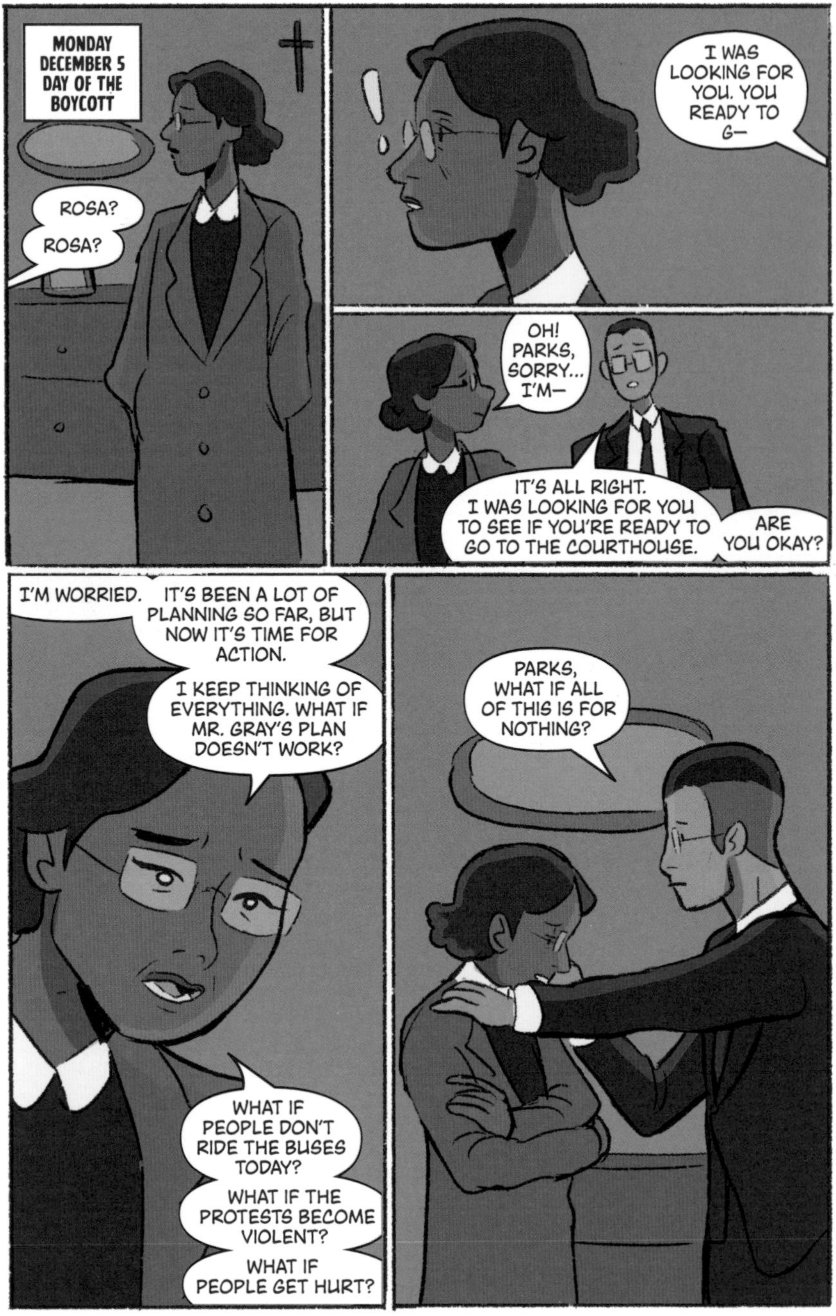
MONDAY
DECEMBER 5
DAY OF THE
BOYCOTT
ROSA?
ROSA?
!
I WAS LOOKING FOR YOU. YOU READY TO G—
OH! PARKS, SORRY... I'M—
IT'S ALL RIGHT. I WAS LOOKING FOR YOU TO SEE IF YOU'RE READY TO GO TO THE COURTHOUSE.
ARE YOU OKAY?
I'M WORRIED.
IT'S BEEN A LOT OF PLANNING SO FAR, BUT NOW IT'S TIME FOR ACTION.
I KEEP THINKING OF EVERYTHING. WHAT IF MR. GRAY'S PLAN DOESN'T WORK?
WHAT IF PEOPLE DON'T RIDE THE BUSES TODAY?
WHAT IF THE PROTESTS BECOME VIOLENT?
WHAT IF PEOPLE GET HURT?
PARKS, WHAT IF ALL OF THIS IS FOR NOTHING?

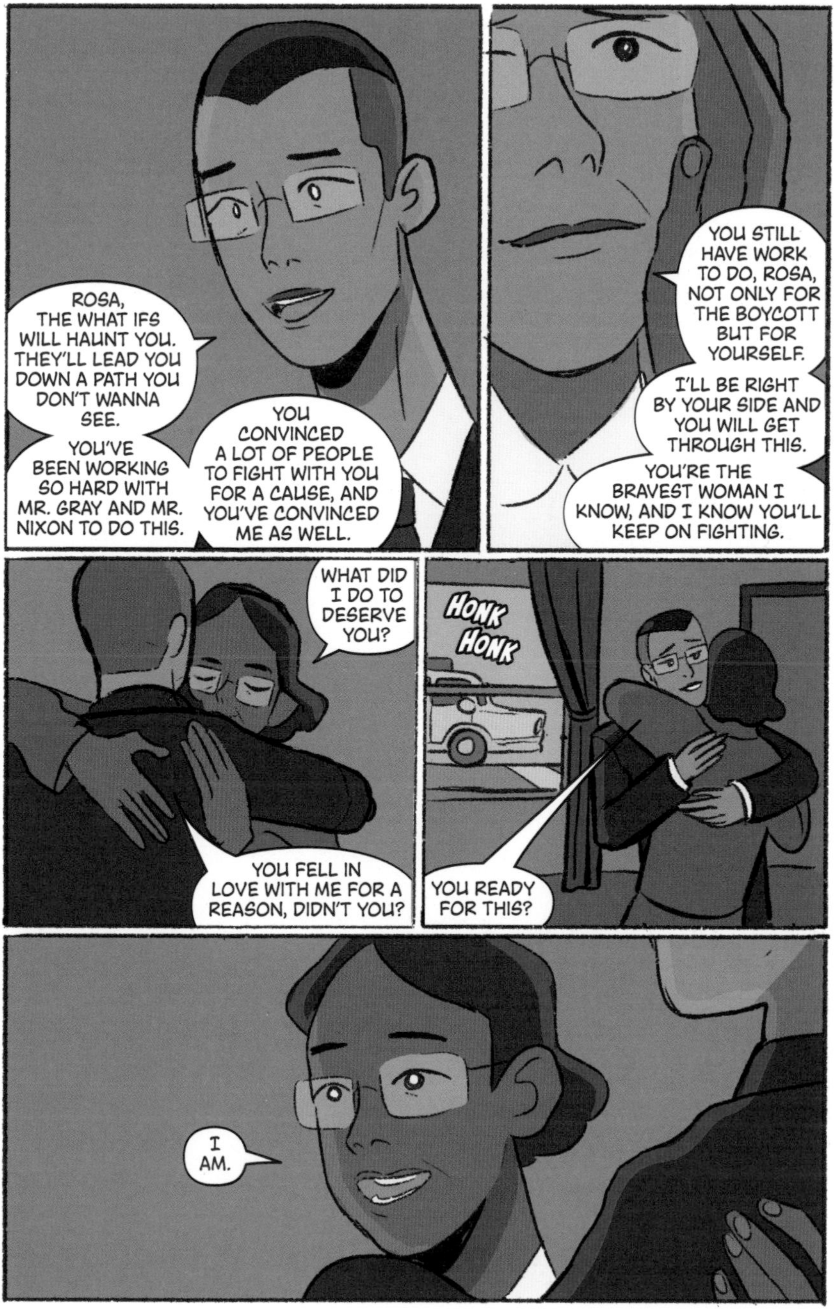
ROSA, THE WHAT IFS WILL HAUNT YOU. THEY'LL LEAD YOU DOWN A PATH YOU DON'T WANNA SEE.
YOU'VE BEEN WORKING SO HARD WITH MR. GRAY AND MR. NIXON TO DO THIS.
YOU CONVINCED A LOT OF PEOPLE TO FIGHT WITH YOU FOR A CAUSE, AND YOU'VE CONVINCED ME AS WELL.
YOU STILL HAVE WORK TO DO, ROSA, NOT ONLY FOR THE BOYCOTT BUT FOR YOURSELF.
I'LL BE RIGHT BY YOUR SIDE AND YOU WILL GET THROUGH THIS.
YOU'RE THE BRAVEST WOMAN I KNOW, AND I KNOW YOU'LL KEEP ON FIGHTING.
WHAT DID I DO TO DESERVE YOU?
YOU FELL IN LOVE WITH ME FOR A REASON, DIDN'T YOU?
HONK
HONK
YOU READY FOR THIS?
I AM.

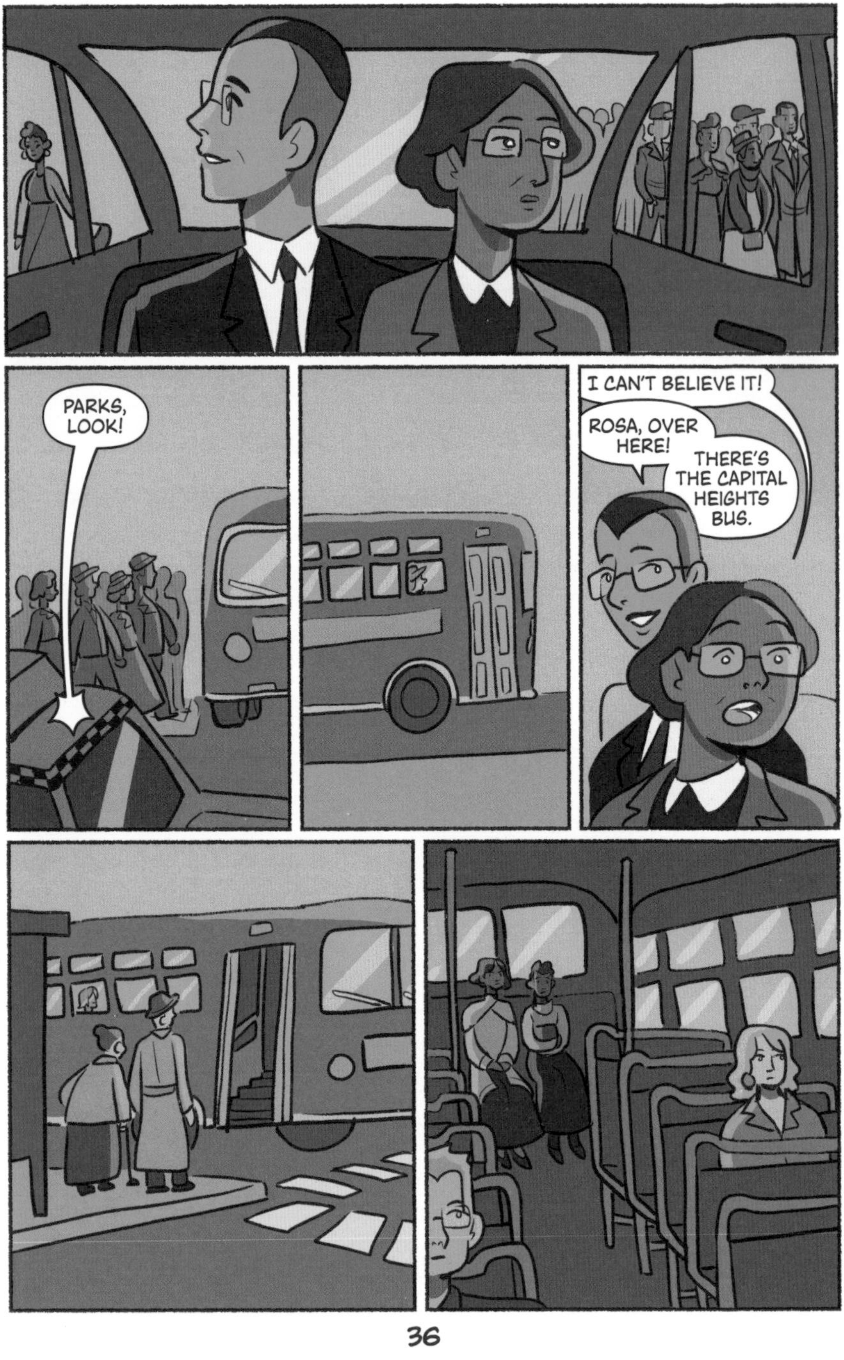
PARKS, LOOK!
I CAN'T BELIEVE IT!
ROSA, OVER HERE!
THERE'S THE CAPITAL HEIGHTS BUS.

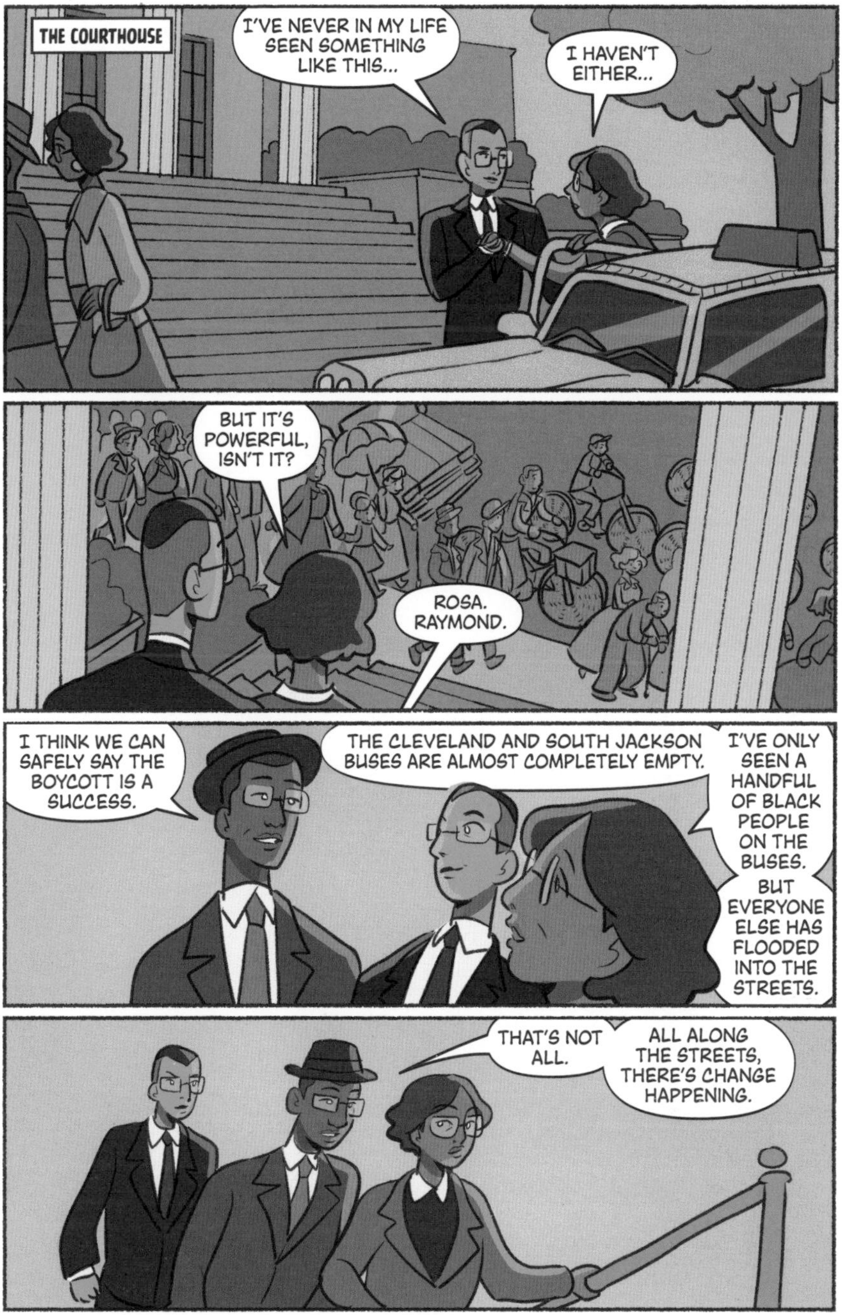
THE COURTHOUSE
I'VE NEVER IN MY LIFE SEEN SOMETHING LIKE THIS...
I HAVEN'T EITHER...
BUT IT'S POWERFUL, ISN'T IT?
ROSA. RAYMOND.
I THINK WE CAN SAFELY SAY THE BOYCOTT IS A SUCCESS.
THE CLEVELAND AND SOUTH JACKSON BUSES ARE ALMOST COMPLETELY EMPTY.
I'VE ONLY SEEN A HANDFUL OF BLACK PEOPLE ON THE BUSES.
BUT EVERYONE ELSE HAS FLOODED INTO THE STREETS.
THAT'S NOT ALL.
ALL ALONG THE STREETS, THERE'S CHANGE HAPPENING.

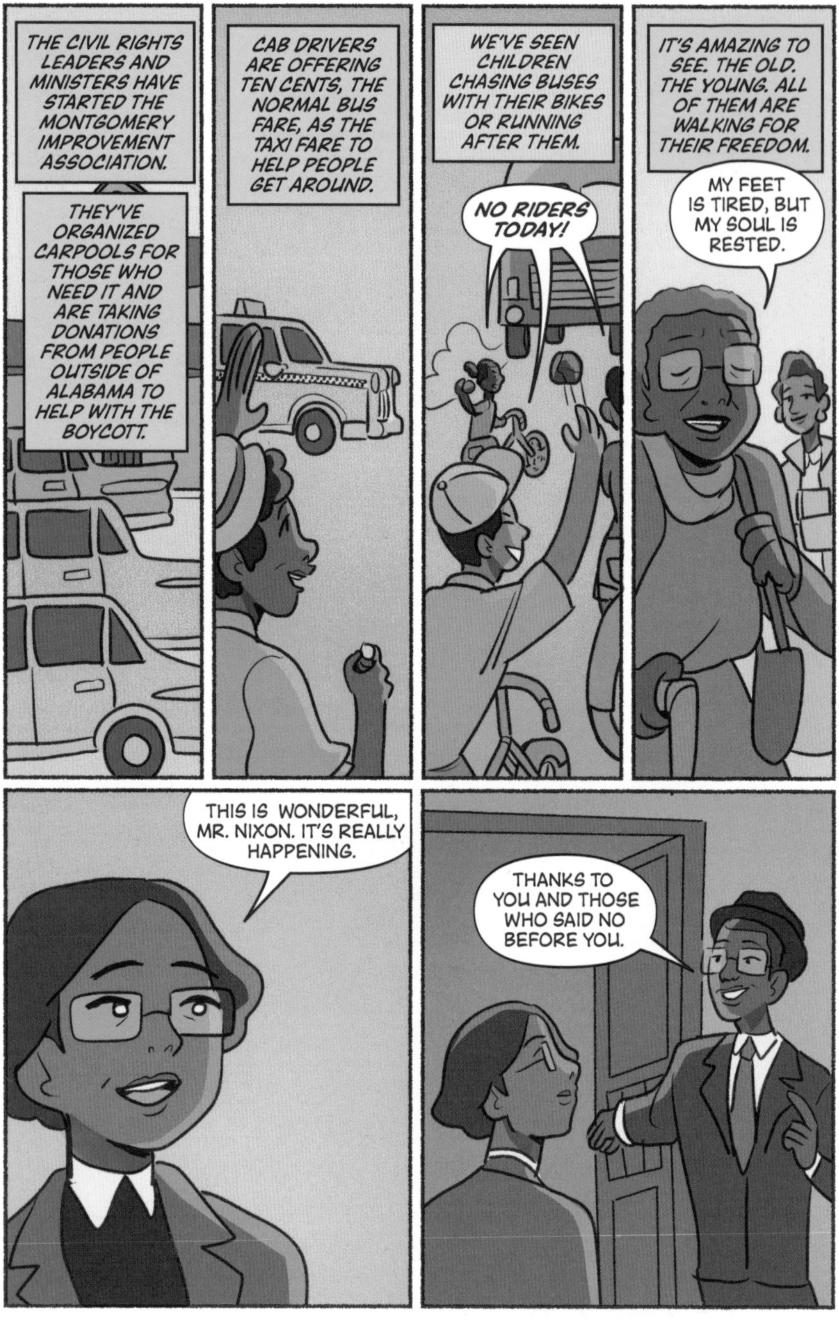

THE CIVIL RIGHTS LEADERS AND MINISTERS HAVE STARTED THE MONTGOMERY IMPROVEMENT ASSOCIATION.
THEY'VE ORGANIZED CARPOOLS FOR THOSE WHO NEED IT AND ARE TAKING DONATIONS FROM PEOPLE OUTSIDE OF ALABAMA TO HELP WITH THE BOYCOTT.
CAB DRIVERS ARE OFFERING TEN CENTS, THE NORMAL BUS FARE, AS THE TAXI FARE TO HELP PEOPLE GET AROUND.
WE'VE SEEN CHILDREN CHASING BUSES WITH THEIR BIKES OR RUNNING AFTER THEM.
NO RIDERS TODAY!
IT'S AMAZING TO SEE. THE OLD. THE YOUNG. ALL OF THEM ARE WALKING FOR THEIR FREEDOM.
MY FEET IS TIRED, BUT MY SOUL IS RESTED.
THIS IS WONDERFUL, MR. NIXON. IT'S REALLY HAPPENING.
THANKS TO YOU AND THOSE WHO SAID NO BEFORE YOU.

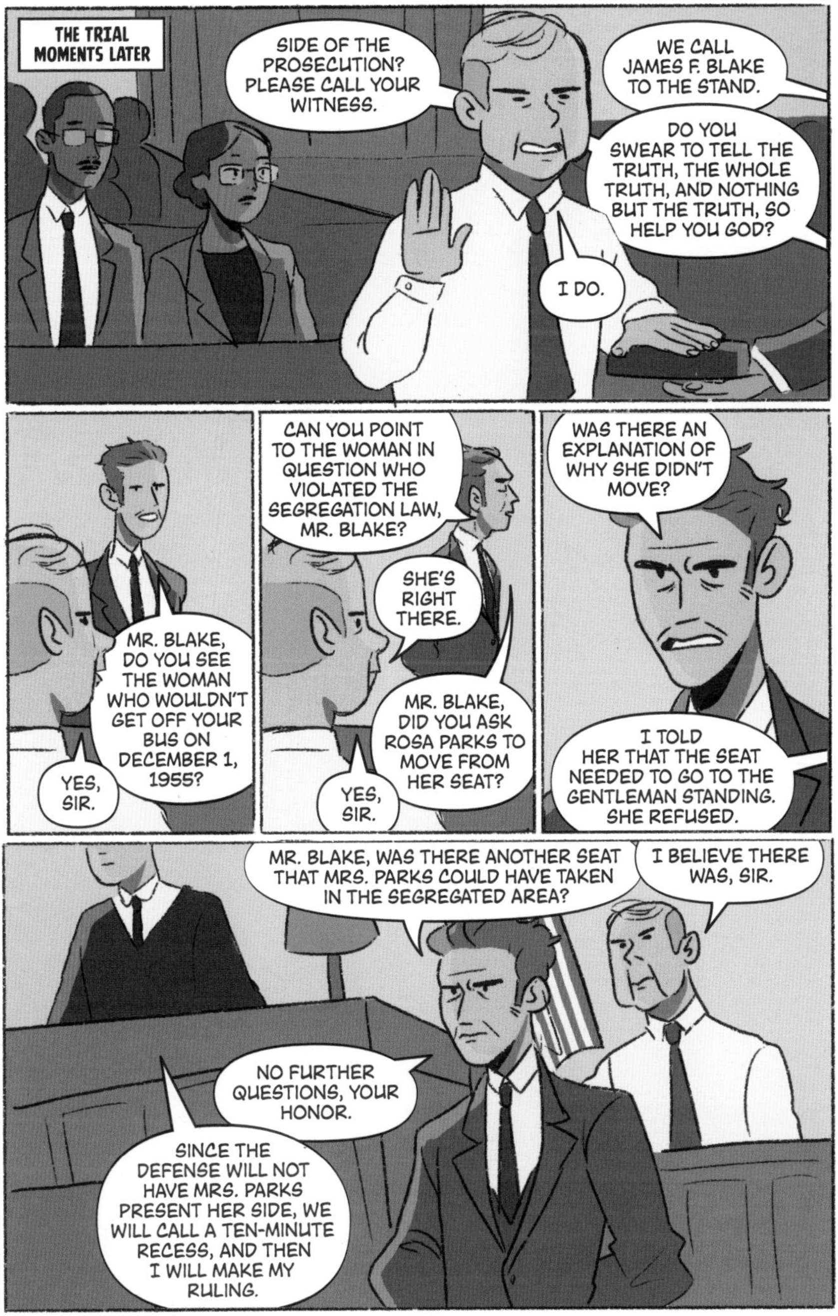
THE TRIAL
MOMENTS LATER
SIDE OF THE PROSECUTION? PLEASE CALL YOUR WITNESS.
WE CALL JAMES F. BLAKE TO THE STAND.
DO YOU SWEAR TO TELL THE TRUTH, THE WHOLE TRUTH, AND NOTHING BUT THE TRUTH, SO HELP YOU GOD?
I DO.
MR. BLAKE, DO YOU SEE THE WOMAN WHO WOULDN'T GET OFF YOUR BUS ON DECEMBER 1, 1955?
YES, SIR.
CAN YOU POINT TO THE WOMAN IN QUESTION WHO VIOLATED THE SEGREGATION LAW, MR. BLAKE?
SHE'S RIGHT THERE.
MR. BLAKE, DID YOU ASK ROSA PARKS TO MOVE FROM HER SEAT?
YES, SIR.
WAS THERE AN EXPLANATION OF WHY SHE DIDN'T MOVE?
I TOLD HER THAT THE SEAT NEEDED TO GO TO THE GENTLEMAN STANDING. SHE REFUSED.
MR. BLAKE, WAS THERE ANOTHER SEAT THAT MRS. PARKS COULD HAVE TAKEN IN THE SEGREGATED AREA?
I BELIEVE THERE WAS, SIR.
NO FURTHER QUESTIONS, YOUR HONOR.
SINCE THE DEFENSE WILL NOT HAVE MRS. PARKS PRESENT HER SIDE, WE WILL CALL A TEN-MINUTE RECESS, AND THEN I WILL MAKE MY RULING.

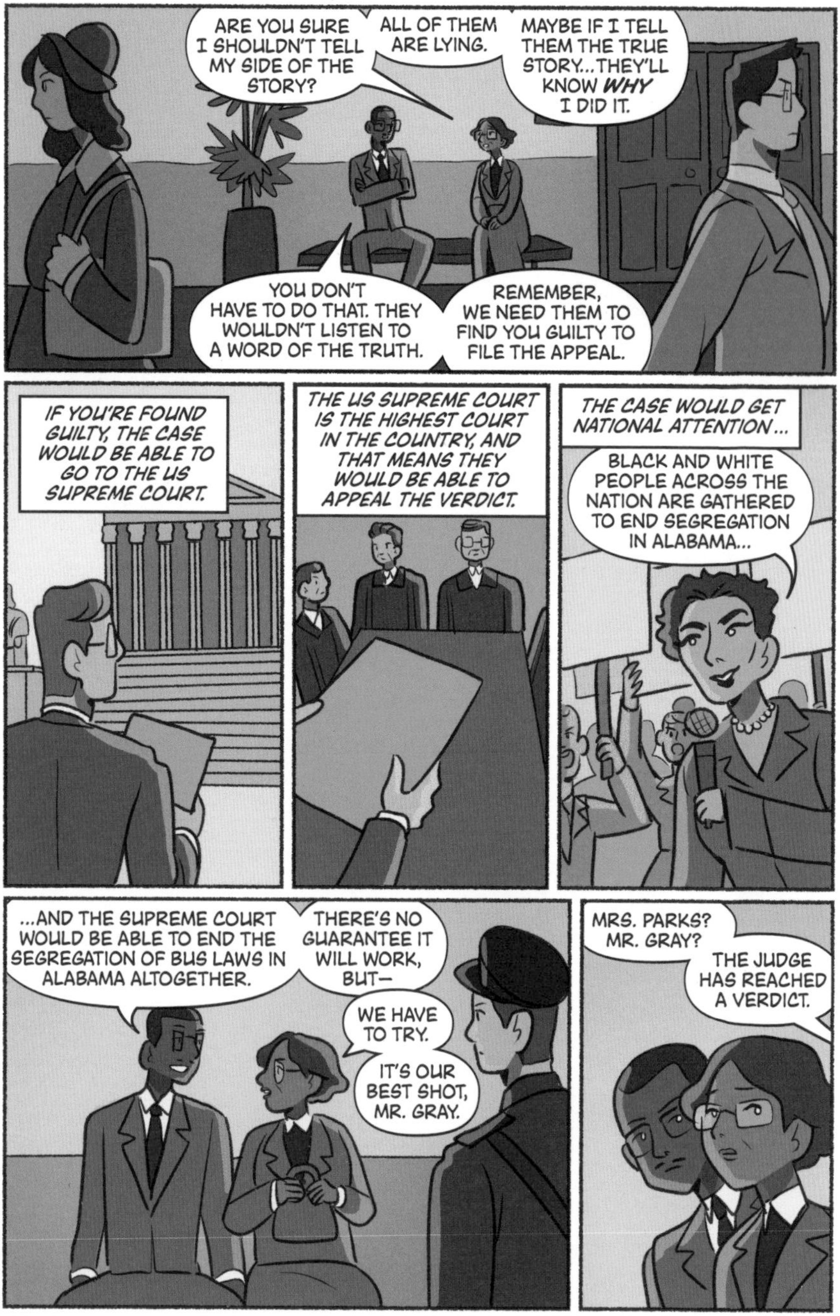
ARE YOU SURE I SHOULDN'T TELL MY SIDE OF THE STORY?
ALL OF THEM ARE LYING.
MAYBE IF I TELL THEM THE TRUE STORY...THEY'LL KNOW WHY I DID IT.
YOU DON'T HAVE TO DO THAT. THEY WOULDN'T LISTEN TO A WORD OF THE TRUTH.
REMEMBER, WE NEED THEM TO FIND YOU GUILTY TO FILE THE APPEAL.
IF YOU'RE FOUND GUILTY, THE CASE WOULD BE ABLE TO GO TO THE US SUPREME COURT.
THE US SUPREME COURT IS THE HIGHEST COURT IN THE COUNTRY, AND THAT MEANS THEY WOULD BE ABLE TO APPEAL THE VERDICT.
THE CASE WOULD GET NATIONAL ATTENTION...
BLACK AND WHITE PEOPLE ACROSS THE NATION ARE GATHERED TO END SEGREGATION IN ALABAMA...
...AND THE SUPREME COURT WOULD BE ABLE TO END THE SEGREGATION OF BUS LAWS IN ALABAMA ALTOGETHER.
THERE'S NO GUARANTEE IT WILL WORK, BUT—
WE HAVE TO TRY.
IT'S OUR BEST SHOT, MR. GRAY.
MRS. PARKS? MR. GRAY?
THE JUDGE HAS REACHED A VERDICT.

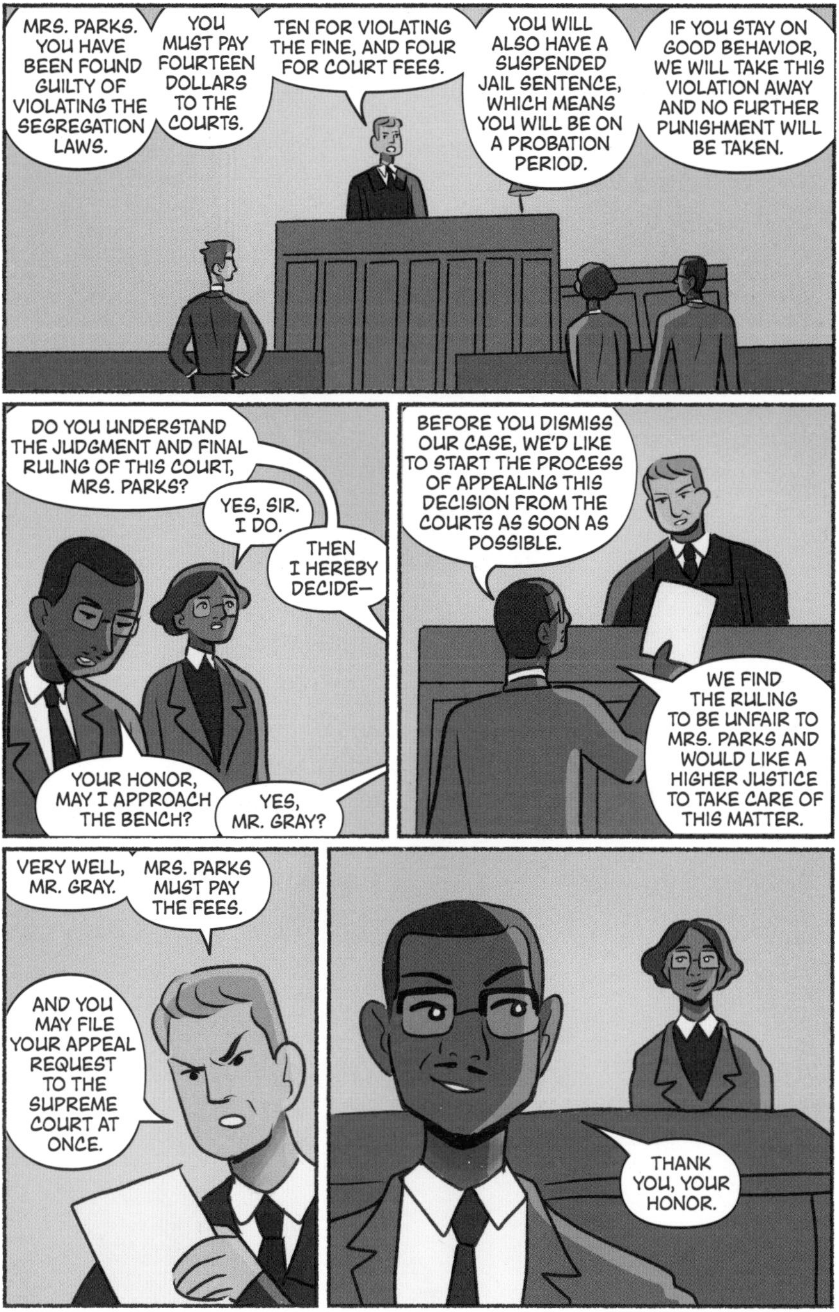
MRS. PARKS. YOU HAVE BEEN FOUND GUILTY OF VIOLATING THE SEGREGATION LAWS.
YOU MUST PAY FOURTEEN DOLLARS TO THE COURTS.
TEN FOR VIOLATING THE FINE, AND FOUR FOR COURT FEES.
YOU WILL ALSO HAVE A SUSPENDED JAIL SENTENCE, WHICH MEANS YOU WILL BE ON A PROBATION PERIOD.
IF YOU STAY ON GOOD BEHAVIOR, WE WILL TAKE THIS VIOLATION AWAY AND NO FURTHER PUNISHMENT WILL BE TAKEN.
DO YOU UNDERSTAND THE JUDGMENT AND FINAL RULING OF THIS COURT, MRS. PARKS?
YES, SIR. I DO.
THEN I HEREBY DECIDE—
YOUR HONOR, MAY I APPROACH THE BENCH?
YES, MR. GRAY?
BEFORE YOU DISMISS OUR CASE, WE'D LIKE TO START THE PROCESS OF APPEALING THIS DECISION FROM THE COURTS AS SOON AS POSSIBLE.
WE FIND THE RULING TO BE UNFAIR TO MRS. PARKS AND WOULD LIKE A HIGHER JUSTICE TO TAKE CARE OF THIS MATTER.
VERY WELL, MR. GRAY.
MRS. PARKS MUST PAY THE FEES.
AND YOU MAY FILE YOUR APPEAL REQUEST TO THE SUPREME COURT AT ONCE.
THANK YOU, YOUR HONOR.

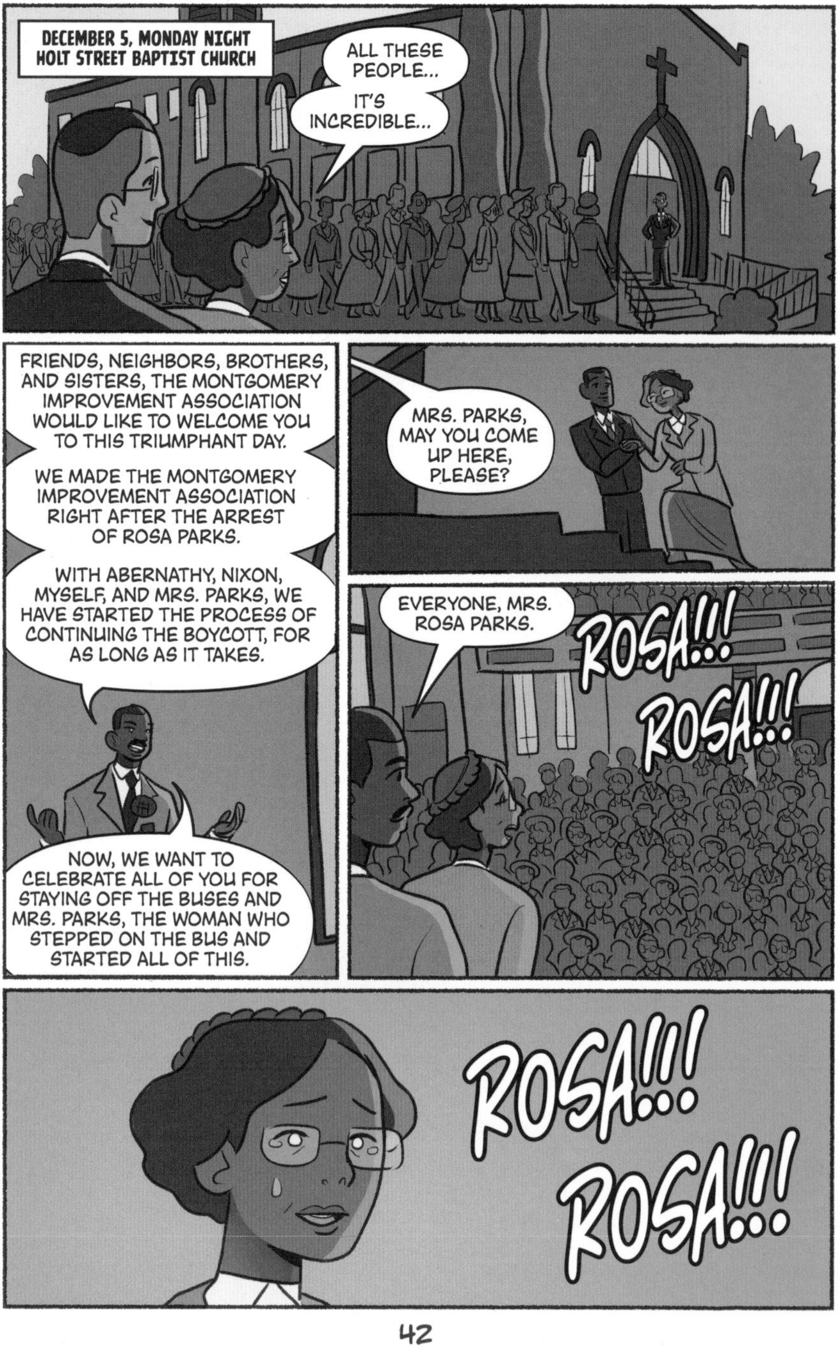
DECEMBER 5, MONDAY NIGHT
HOLT STREET BAPTIST CHURCH
ALL THESE PEOPLE...
IT'S INCREDIBLE...
FRIENDS, NEIGHBORS, BROTHERS, AND SISTERS, THE MONTGOMERY IMPROVEMENT ASSOCIATION WOULD LIKE TO WELCOME YOU TO THIS TRIUMPHANT DAY.
WE MADE THE MONTGOMERY IMPROVEMENT ASSOCIATION RIGHT AFTER THE ARREST OF ROSA PARKS.
WITH ABERNATHY, NIXON, MYSELF, AND MRS. PARKS, WE HAVE STARTED THE PROCESS OF CONTINUING THE BOYCOTT, FOR AS LONG AS IT TAKES.
NOW, WE WANT TO CELEBRATE ALL OF YOU FOR STAYING OFF THE BUSES AND MRS. PARKS, THE WOMAN WHO STEPPED ON THE BUS AND STARTED ALL OF THIS.
MRS. PARKS, MAY YOU COME UP HERE, PLEASE?
EVERYONE, MRS. ROSA PARKS.
ROSA!!!
ROSA!!!
ROSA!!!
ROSA!!!

Montgomery Improvement Association

The Montgomery Improvement Association, or MIA, was one of the leading organizations in supporting the Montgomery Bus Boycott. Led by Martin Luther King Jr., the MIA was made up of eighteen members and used a nonviolent approach to protest segregation.

The Montgomery Improvement Association helped keep Montgomery informed of what was happening during the boycott. They raised money and collected donated items for protestors, including shoes for those who wore out the soles of theirs from walking. They provided carpooling, which worked as a taxi-like system. Church vans and privately owned vehicles helped anyone get around where they needed to go.

The organization continued to provide help to Black people in Montgomery after the boycott ended. They coordinated people to vote and tried to end segregation in many local schools, parks, and other facilities that Black people weren't allowed to go to. In 1957, the MIA slowly dissolved, but gave way to the Southern Christian Leadership Conference, an organization that still continues to do civil rights work today.

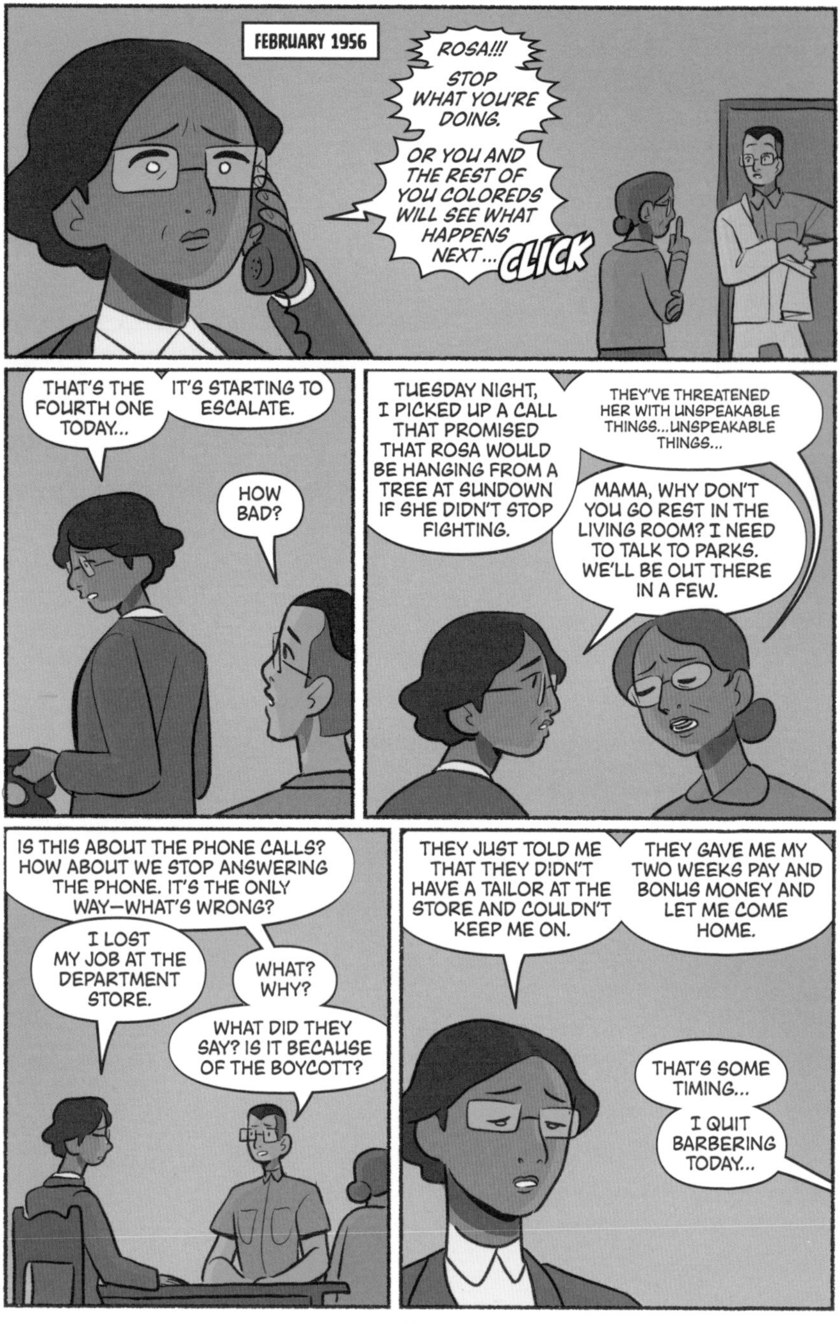
FEBRUARY 1956
ROSA!!! STOP WHAT YOU'RE DOING. OR YOU AND THE REST OF YOU COLOREDS WILL SEE WHAT HAPPENS NEXT...
CLICK
THAT'S THE FOURTH ONE TODAY...
IT'S STARTING TO ESCALATE.
HOW BAD?
TUESDAY NIGHT, I PICKED UP A CALL THAT PROMISED THAT ROSA WOULD BE HANGING FROM A TREE AT SUNDOWN IF SHE DIDN'T STOP FIGHTING.
THEY'VE THREATENED HER WITH UNSPEAKABLE THINGS...UNSPEAKABLE THINGS...
MAMA, WHY DON'T YOU GO REST IN THE LIVING ROOM? I NEED TO TALK TO PARKS. WE'LL BE OUT THERE IN A FEW.
IS THIS ABOUT THE PHONE CALLS? HOW ABOUT WE STOP ANSWERING THE PHONE. IT'S THE ONLY WAY—WHAT'S WRONG?
I LOST MY JOB AT THE DEPARTMENT STORE.
WHAT? WHY?
WHAT DID THEY SAY? IS IT BECAUSE OF THE BOYCOTT?
THEY JUST TOLD ME THAT THEY DIDN'T HAVE A TAILOR AT THE STORE AND COULDN'T KEEP ME ON.
THEY GAVE ME MY TWO WEEKS PAY AND BONUS MONEY AND LET ME COME HOME.
THAT'S SOME TIMING...
I QUIT BARBERING TODAY...

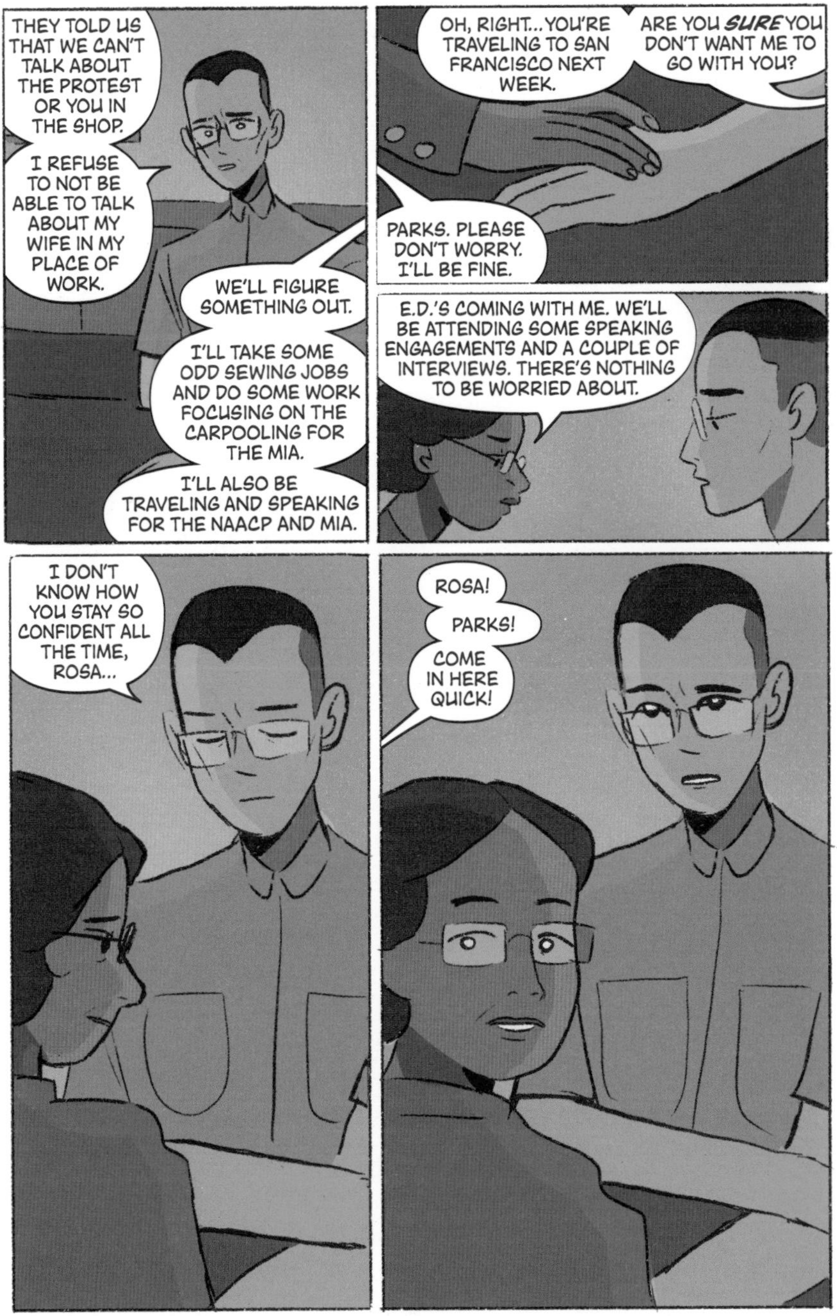
THEY TOLD US THAT WE CAN'T TALK ABOUT THE PROTEST OR YOU IN THE SHOP.
I REFUSE TO NOT BE ABLE TO TALK ABOUT MY WIFE IN MY PLACE OF WORK.
WE'LL FIGURE SOMETHING OUT.
I'LL TAKE SOME ODD SEWING JOBS AND DO SOME WORK FOCUSING ON THE CARPOOLING FOR THE MIA.
I'LL ALSO BE TRAVELING AND SPEAKING FOR THE NAACP AND MIA.
OH, RIGHT... YOU'RE TRAVELING TO SAN FRANCISCO NEXT WEEK.
ARE YOU SURE YOU DON'T WANT ME TO GO WITH YOU?
PARKS. PLEASE DON'T WORRY. I'LL BE FINE.
E.D.'S COMING WITH ME. WE'LL BE ATTENDING SOME SPEAKING ENGAGEMENTS AND A COUPLE OF INTERVIEWS. THERE'S NOTHING TO BE WORRIED ABOUT.
I DON'T KNOW HOW YOU STAY SO CONFIDENT ALL THE TIME, ROSA...
ROSA!
PARKS!
COME IN HERE QUICK!

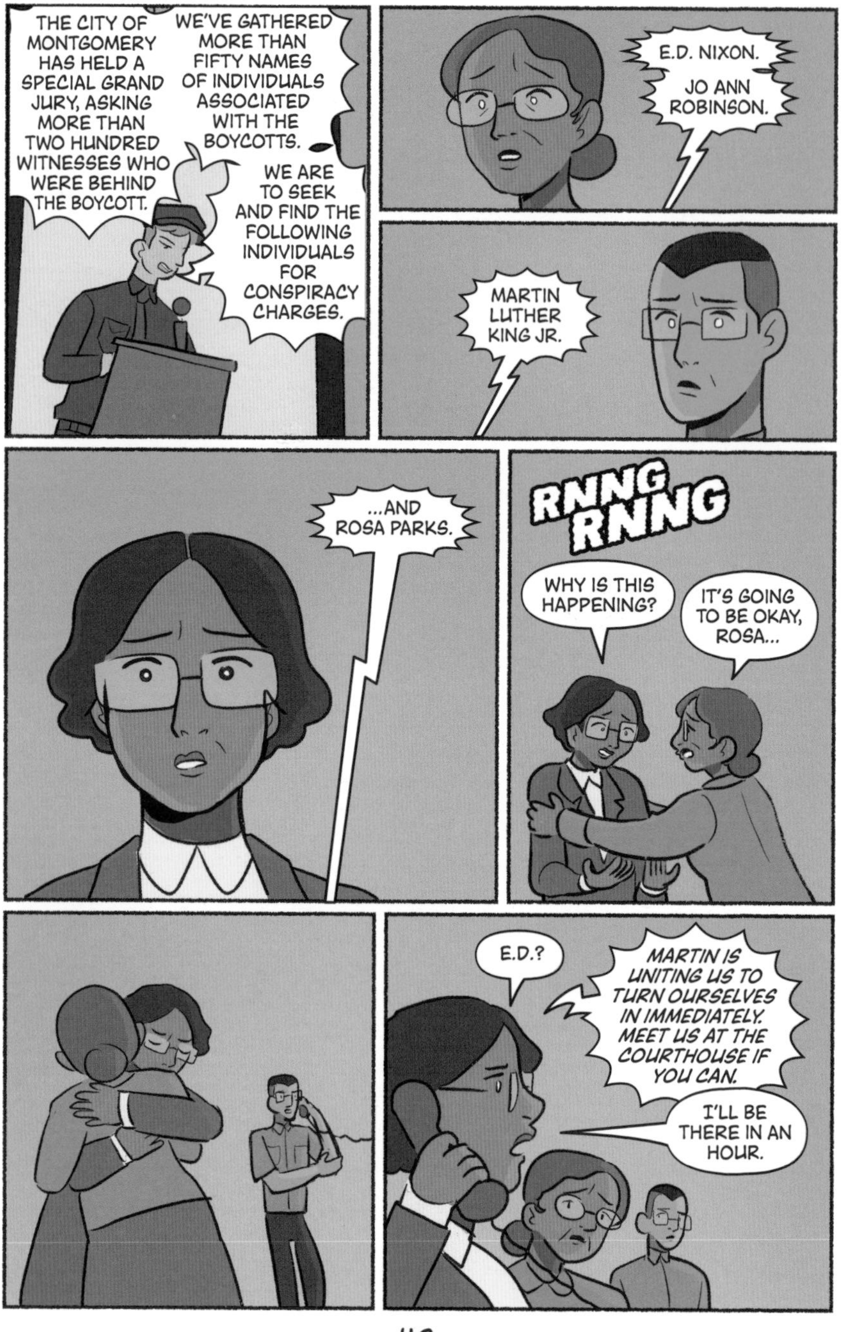
THE CITY OF MONTGOMERY HAS HELD A SPECIAL GRAND JURY, ASKING MORE THAN TWO HUNDRED WITNESSES WHO WERE BEHIND THE BOYCOTT.
WE'VE GATHERED MORE THAN FIFTY NAMES OF INDIVIDUALS ASSOCIATED WITH THE BOYCOTTS.
WE ARE TO SEEK AND FIND THE FOLLOWING INDIVIDUALS FOR CONSPIRACY CHARGES.
E.D. NIXON.
JO ANN ROBINSON.
MARTIN LUTHER KING JR.
...AND ROSA PARKS.
RNNG RNNG
WHY IS THIS HAPPENING?
IT'S GOING TO BE OKAY, ROSA...
E.D.?
MARTIN IS UNITING US TO TURN OURSELVES IN IMMEDIATELY. MEET US AT THE COURTHOUSE IF YOU CAN.
I'LL BE THERE IN AN HOUR.

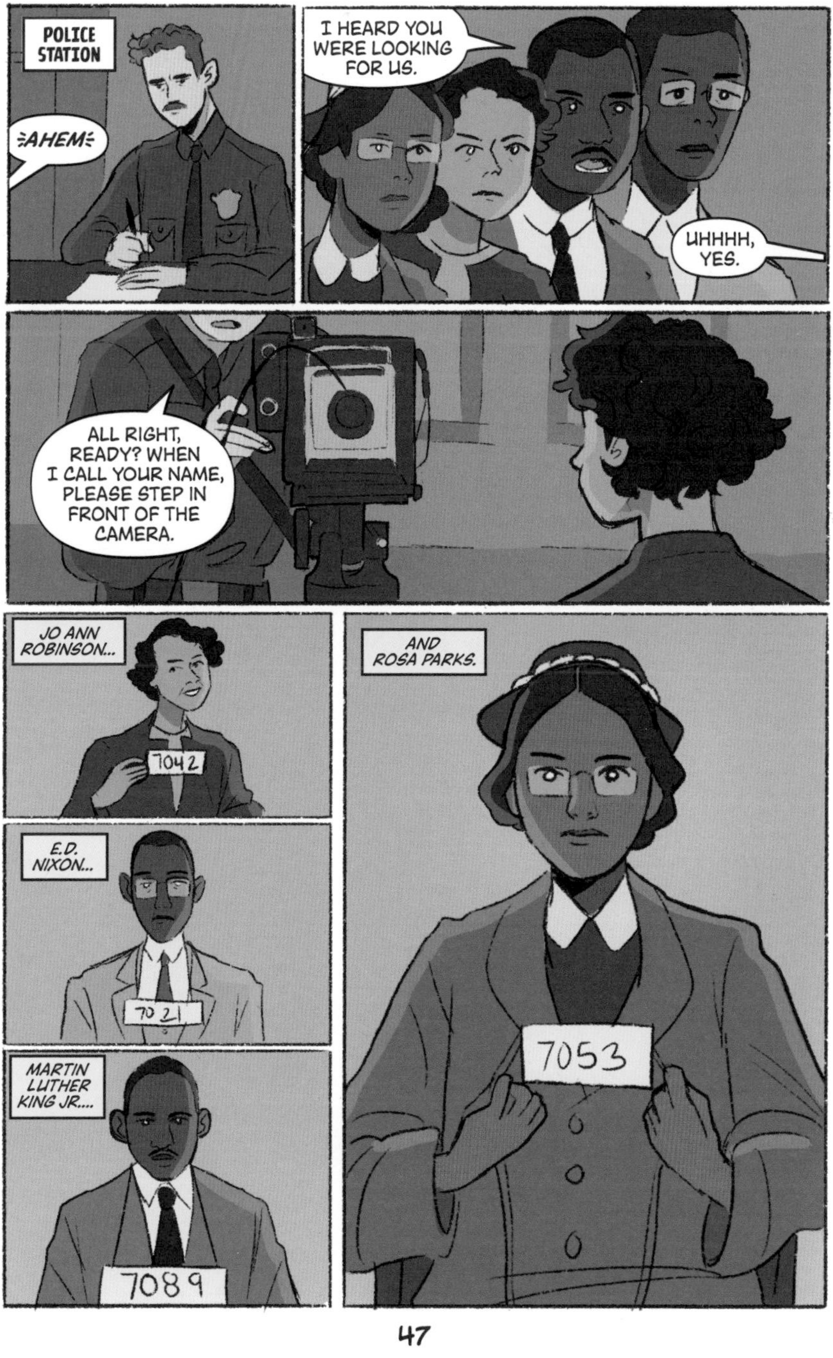
POLICE STATION
AHEM
I HEARD YOU WERE LOOKING FOR US.
UHHHH, YES.
ALL RIGHT, READY? WHEN I CALL YOUR NAME, PLEASE STEP IN FRONT OF THE CAMERA.
JO ANN ROBINSON...
7042
E.D. NIXON...
7021
MARTIN LUTHER KING JR....
7089
AND ROSA PARKS.
7053

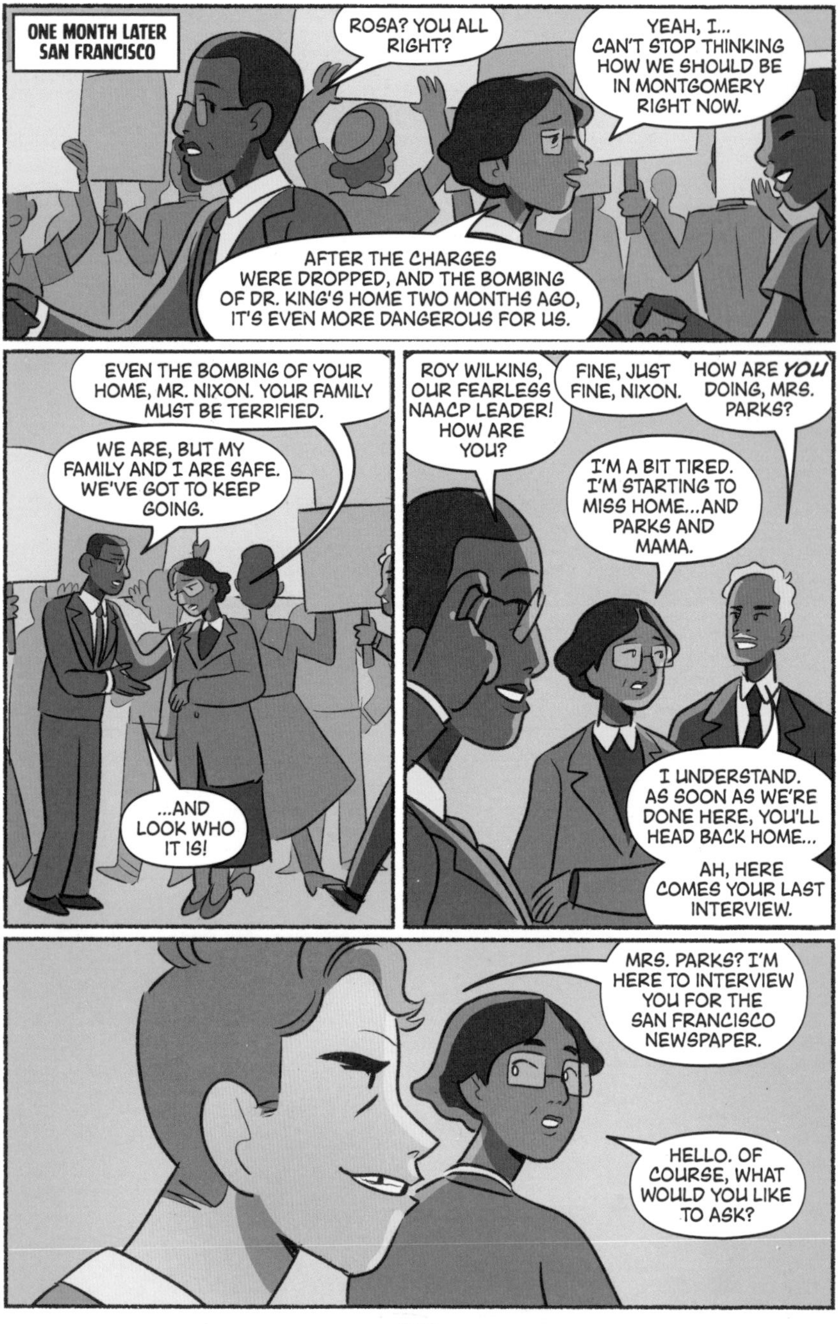
ONE MONTH LATER SAN FRANCISCO
ROSA? YOU ALL RIGHT?
YEAH, I... CAN'T STOP THINKING HOW WE SHOULD BE IN MONTGOMERY RIGHT NOW.
AFTER THE CHARGES WERE DROPPED, AND THE BOMBING OF DR. KING'S HOME TWO MONTHS AGO, IT'S EVEN MORE DANGEROUS FOR US.
EVEN THE BOMBING OF YOUR HOME, MR. NIXON. YOUR FAMILY MUST BE TERRIFIED.
WE ARE, BUT MY FAMILY AND I ARE SAFE. WE'VE GOT TO KEEP GOING.
...AND LOOK WHO IT IS!
ROY WILKINS, OUR FEARLESS NAACP LEADER! HOW ARE YOU?
FINE, JUST FINE, NIXON.
HOW ARE *YOU* DOING, MRS. PARKS?
I'M A BIT TIRED. I'M STARTING TO MISS HOME...AND PARKS AND MAMA.
I UNDERSTAND. AS SOON AS WE'RE DONE HERE, YOU'LL HEAD BACK HOME...
AH, HERE COMES YOUR LAST INTERVIEW.
MRS. PARKS? I'M HERE TO INTERVIEW YOU FOR THE SAN FRANCISCO NEWSPAPER.
HELLO. OF COURSE, WHAT WOULD YOU LIKE TO ASK?

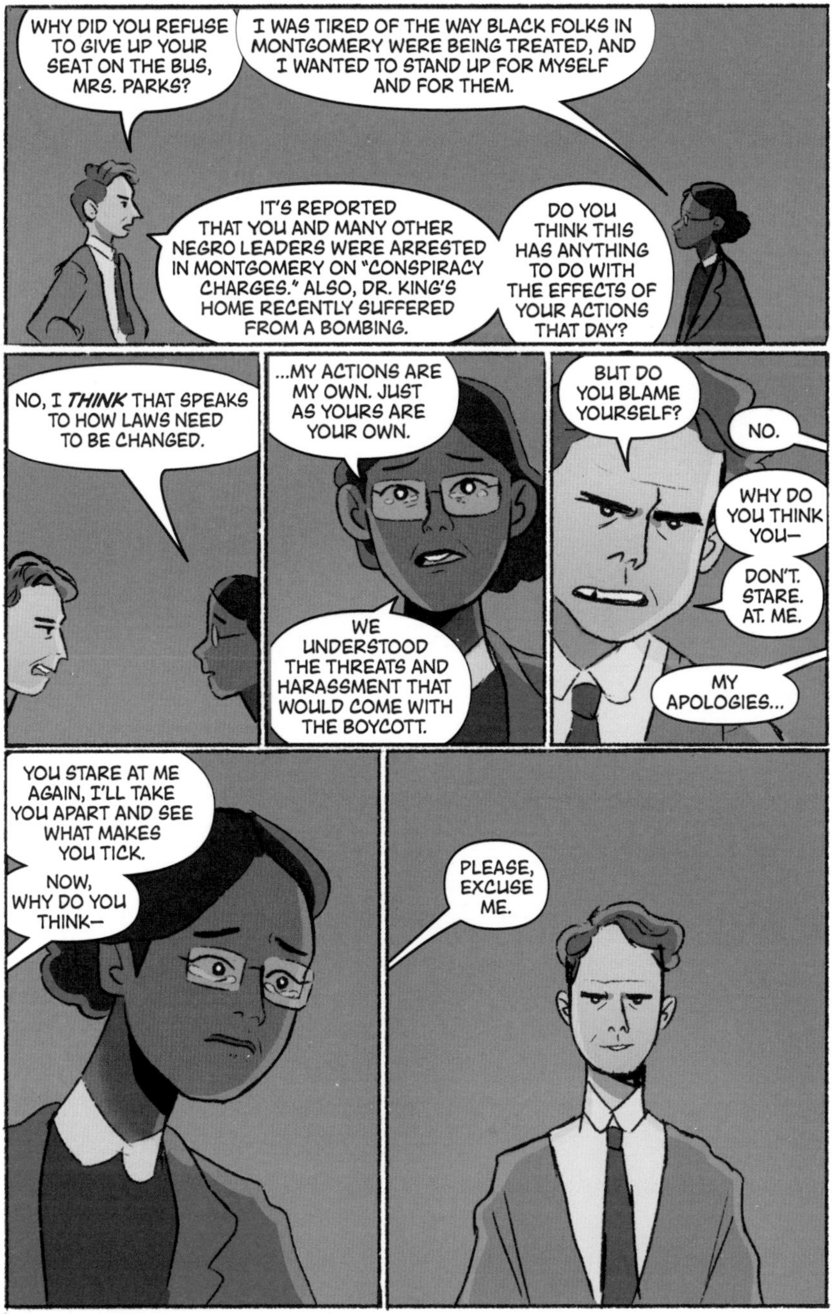
WHY DID YOU REFUSE TO GIVE UP YOUR SEAT ON THE BUS, MRS. PARKS?
I WAS TIRED OF THE WAY BLACK FOLKS IN MONTGOMERY WERE BEING TREATED, AND I WANTED TO STAND UP FOR MYSELF AND FOR THEM.
IT'S REPORTED THAT YOU AND MANY OTHER NEGRO LEADERS WERE ARRESTED IN MONTGOMERY ON "CONSPIRACY CHARGES." ALSO, DR. KING'S HOME RECENTLY SUFFERED FROM A BOMBING.
DO YOU THINK THIS HAS ANYTHING TO DO WITH THE EFFECTS OF YOUR ACTIONS THAT DAY?
NO, I *THINK* THAT SPEAKS TO HOW LAWS NEED TO BE CHANGED.
...MY ACTIONS ARE MY OWN. JUST AS YOURS ARE YOUR OWN.
WE UNDERSTOOD THE THREATS AND HARASSMENT THAT WOULD COME WITH THE BOYCOTT.
BUT DO YOU BLAME YOURSELF?
NO.
WHY DO YOU THINK YOU—
DON'T. STARE. AT. ME.
MY APOLOGIES...
YOU STARE AT ME AGAIN, I'LL TAKE YOU APART AND SEE WHAT MAKES YOU TICK.
NOW, WHY DO YOU THINK—
PLEASE, EXCUSE ME.

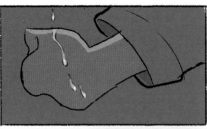

I'M SO SORRY, ROY...I'M SUPPOSED TO BE STRONG.

I'M SORRY...

I CAN GET THROUGH THE INTERVIEW. I JUST NEED TIME...

IT'S ALL RIGHT, ROSA...

IT'S ALL RIGHT.

⧧SOBS⧧

⧧SOBS⧧

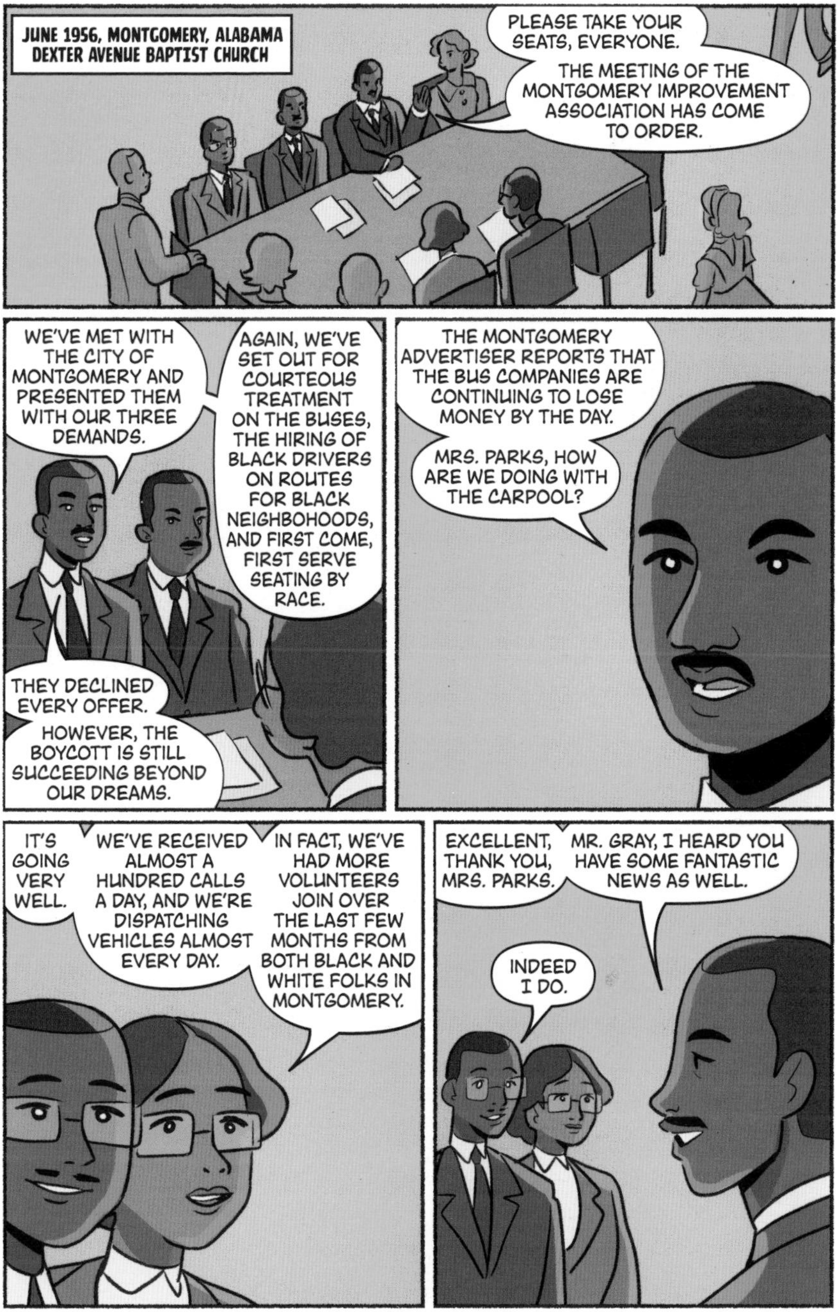
JUNE 1956, MONTGOMERY, ALABAMA
DEXTER AVENUE BAPTIST CHURCH
PLEASE TAKE YOUR SEATS, EVERYONE.
THE MEETING OF THE MONTGOMERY IMPROVEMENT ASSOCIATION HAS COME TO ORDER.
WE'VE MET WITH THE CITY OF MONTGOMERY AND PRESENTED THEM WITH OUR THREE DEMANDS.
AGAIN, WE'VE SET OUT FOR COURTEOUS TREATMENT ON THE BUSES, THE HIRING OF BLACK DRIVERS ON ROUTES FOR BLACK NEIGHBOHOODS, AND FIRST COME, FIRST SERVE SEATING BY RACE.
THEY DECLINED EVERY OFFER.
HOWEVER, THE BOYCOTT IS STILL SUCCEEDING BEYOND OUR DREAMS.
THE MONTGOMERY ADVERTISER REPORTS THAT THE BUS COMPANIES ARE CONTINUING TO LOSE MONEY BY THE DAY.
MRS. PARKS, HOW ARE WE DOING WITH THE CARPOOL?
IT'S GOING VERY WELL.
WE'VE RECEIVED ALMOST A HUNDRED CALLS A DAY, AND WE'RE DISPATCHING VEHICLES ALMOST EVERY DAY.
IN FACT, WE'VE HAD MORE VOLUNTEERS JOIN OVER THE LAST FEW MONTHS FROM BOTH BLACK AND WHITE FOLKS IN MONTGOMERY.
EXCELLENT, THANK YOU, MRS. PARKS.
MR. GRAY, I HEARD YOU HAVE SOME FANTASTIC NEWS AS WELL.
INDEED I DO.

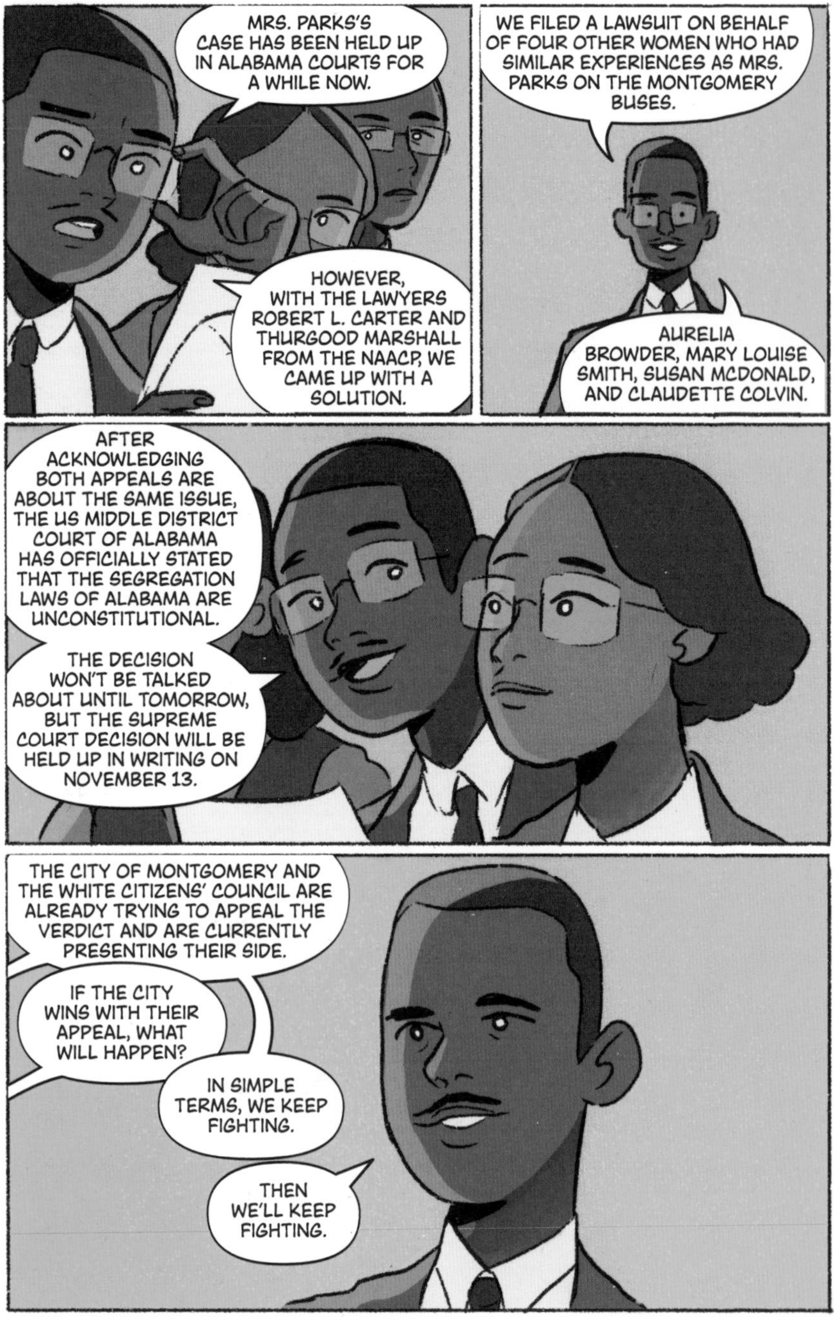
MRS. PARKS'S CASE HAS BEEN HELD UP IN ALABAMA COURTS FOR A WHILE NOW.
HOWEVER, WITH THE LAWYERS ROBERT L. CARTER AND THURGOOD MARSHALL FROM THE NAACP, WE CAME UP WITH A SOLUTION.
WE FILED A LAWSUIT ON BEHALF OF FOUR OTHER WOMEN WHO HAD SIMILAR EXPERIENCES AS MRS. PARKS ON THE MONTGOMERY BUSES.
AURELIA BROWDER, MARY LOUISE SMITH, SUSAN MCDONALD, AND CLAUDETTE COLVIN.
AFTER ACKNOWLEDGING BOTH APPEALS ARE ABOUT THE SAME ISSUE, THE US MIDDLE DISTRICT COURT OF ALABAMA HAS OFFICIALLY STATED THAT THE SEGREGATION LAWS OF ALABAMA ARE UNCONSTITUTIONAL.
THE DECISION WON'T BE TALKED ABOUT UNTIL TOMORROW, BUT THE SUPREME COURT DECISION WILL BE HELD UP IN WRITING ON NOVEMBER 13.
THE CITY OF MONTGOMERY AND THE WHITE CITIZENS' COUNCIL ARE ALREADY TRYING TO APPEAL THE VERDICT AND ARE CURRENTLY PRESENTING THEIR SIDE.
IF THE CITY WINS WITH THEIR APPEAL, WHAT WILL HAPPEN?
IN SIMPLE TERMS, WE KEEP FIGHTING.
THEN WE'LL KEEP FIGHTING.

Claudette Colvin

Born on September 5, 1939, Claudette Colvin is a retired nurse aid and civil rights leader who grew up in Montgomery, Alabama. From a young age, Claudette had a particular interest in activism. She was a good, curious student and an active member of the NAACP youth council.

On March 2, 1955, Claudette, who was fifteen at the time, was arrested for not giving up her seat on a crowded bus to a white passenger. The NAACP thought about representing Claudette as a test case in court, but decided against it because, not long before her court date, she became pregnant. Claudette went to court by herself and was found guilty of violating segregation laws. The courts sentenced her to probation.

In 1956, Colvin became one of the four plaintiffs in the case of *Browder v. Gayle*, which protested segregation on buses in Montgomery, Alabama. Claudette was vital in organizing the fight against segregation during the civil rights movement.

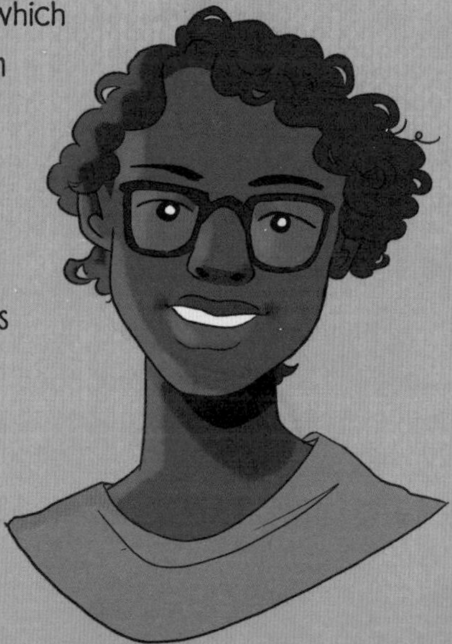

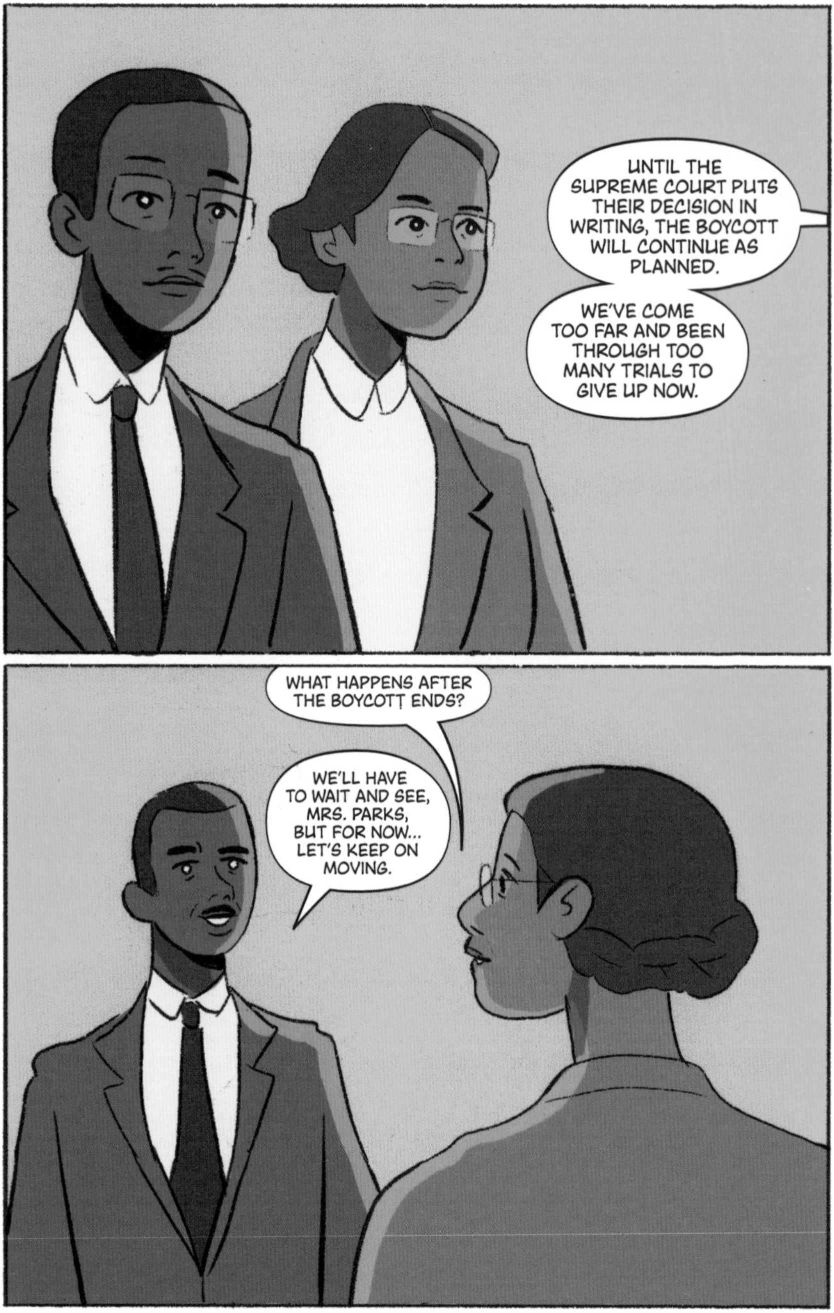
UNTIL THE SUPREME COURT PUTS THEIR DECISION IN WRITING, THE BOYCOTT WILL CONTINUE AS PLANNED.
WE'VE COME TOO FAR AND BEEN THROUGH TOO MANY TRIALS TO GIVE UP NOW.
WHAT HAPPENS AFTER THE BOYCOTT ENDS?
WE'LL HAVE TO WAIT AND SEE, MRS. PARKS, BUT FOR NOW... LET'S KEEP ON MOVING.

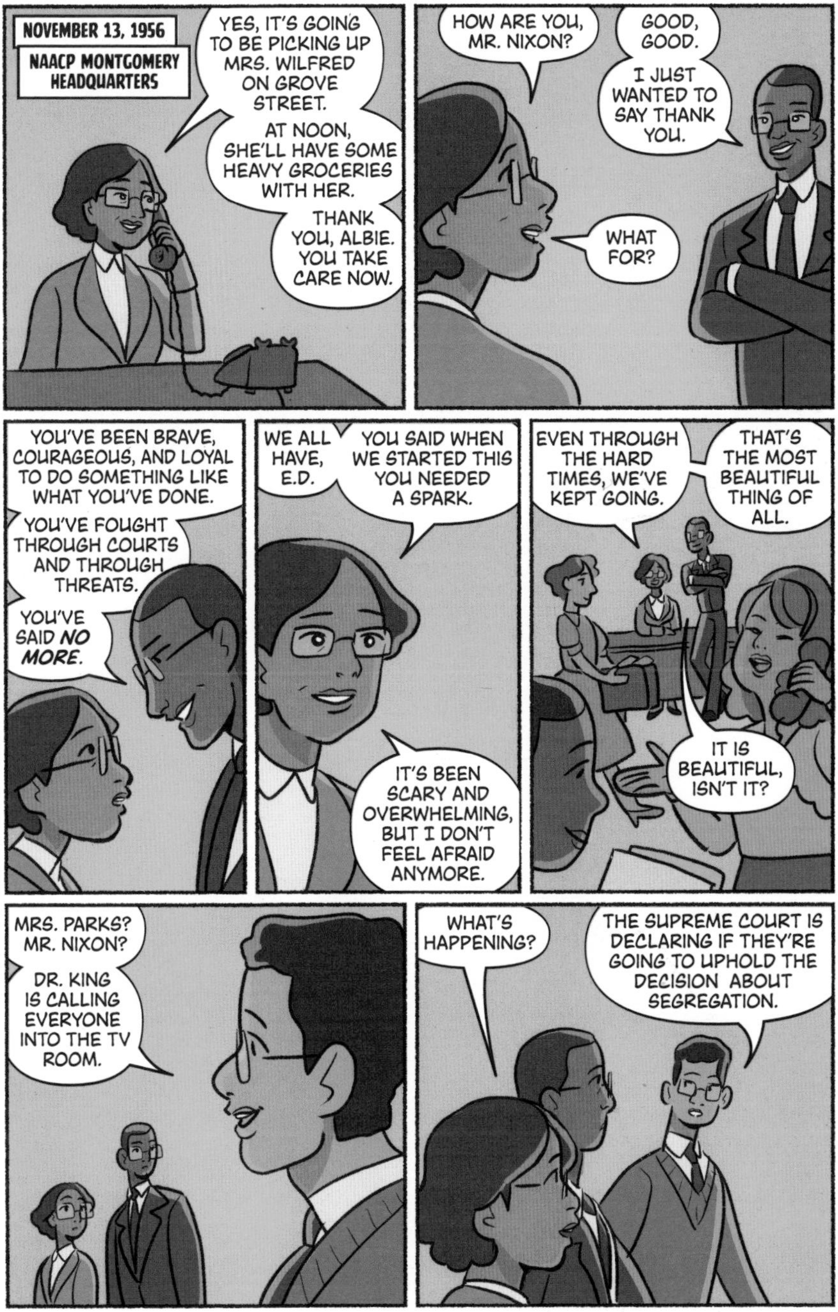
NOVEMBER 13, 1956
NAACP MONTGOMERY HEADQUARTERS
YES, IT'S GOING TO BE PICKING UP MRS. WILFRED ON GROVE STREET.
AT NOON, SHE'LL HAVE SOME HEAVY GROCERIES WITH HER.
THANK YOU, ALBIE. YOU TAKE CARE NOW.
HOW ARE YOU, MR. NIXON?
GOOD, GOOD.
I JUST WANTED TO SAY THANK YOU.
WHAT FOR?
YOU'VE BEEN BRAVE, COURAGEOUS, AND LOYAL TO DO SOMETHING LIKE WHAT YOU'VE DONE.
YOU'VE FOUGHT THROUGH COURTS AND THROUGH THREATS.
YOU'VE SAID *NO MORE*.
WE ALL HAVE, E.D.
YOU SAID WHEN WE STARTED THIS YOU NEEDED A SPARK.
IT'S BEEN SCARY AND OVERWHELMING, BUT I DON'T FEEL AFRAID ANYMORE.
EVEN THROUGH THE HARD TIMES, WE'VE KEPT GOING.
THAT'S THE MOST BEAUTIFUL THING OF ALL.
IT IS BEAUTIFUL, ISN'T IT?
MRS. PARKS? MR. NIXON?
DR. KING IS CALLING EVERYONE INTO THE TV ROOM.
WHAT'S HAPPENING?
THE SUPREME COURT IS DECLARING IF THEY'RE GOING TO UPHOLD THE DECISION ABOUT SEGREGATION.

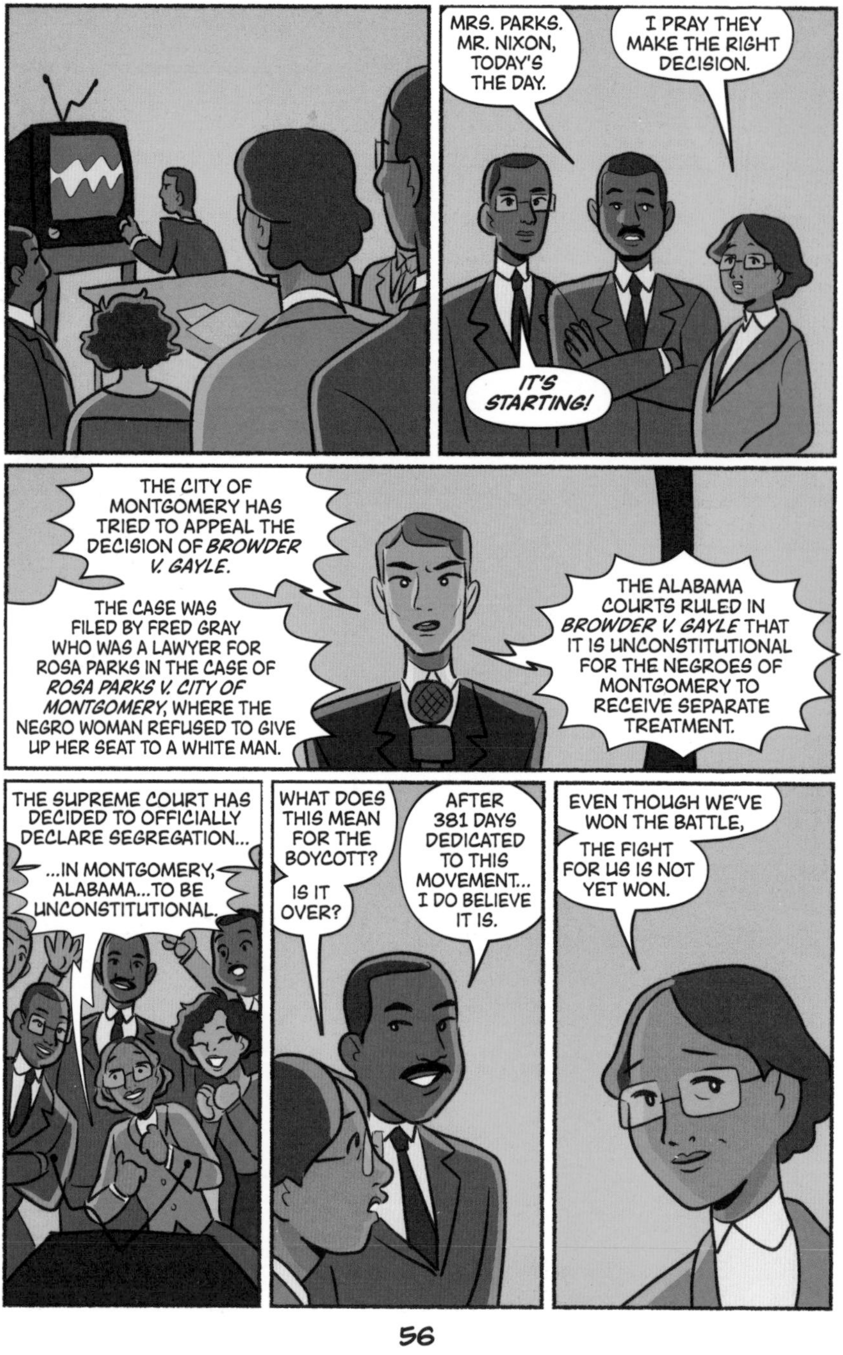
MRS. PARKS. MR. NIXON, TODAY'S THE DAY.
I PRAY THEY MAKE THE RIGHT DECISION.
IT'S STARTING!
THE CITY OF MONTGOMERY HAS TRIED TO APPEAL THE DECISION OF *BROWDER V. GAYLE*.
THE CASE WAS FILED BY FRED GRAY WHO WAS A LAWYER FOR ROSA PARKS IN THE CASE OF *ROSA PARKS V. CITY OF MONTGOMERY*, WHERE THE NEGRO WOMAN REFUSED TO GIVE UP HER SEAT TO A WHITE MAN.
THE ALABAMA COURTS RULED IN *BROWDER V. GAYLE* THAT IT IS UNCONSTITUTIONAL FOR THE NEGROES OF MONTGOMERY TO RECEIVE SEPARATE TREATMENT.
THE SUPREME COURT HAS DECIDED TO OFFICIALLY DECLARE SEGREGATION...
...IN MONTGOMERY, ALABAMA...TO BE UNCONSTITUTIONAL.
WHAT DOES THIS MEAN FOR THE BOYCOTT?
IS IT OVER?
AFTER 381 DAYS DEDICATED TO THIS MOVEMENT... I DO BELIEVE IT IS.
EVEN THOUGH WE'VE WON THE BATTLE,
THE FIGHT FOR US IS NOT YET WON.

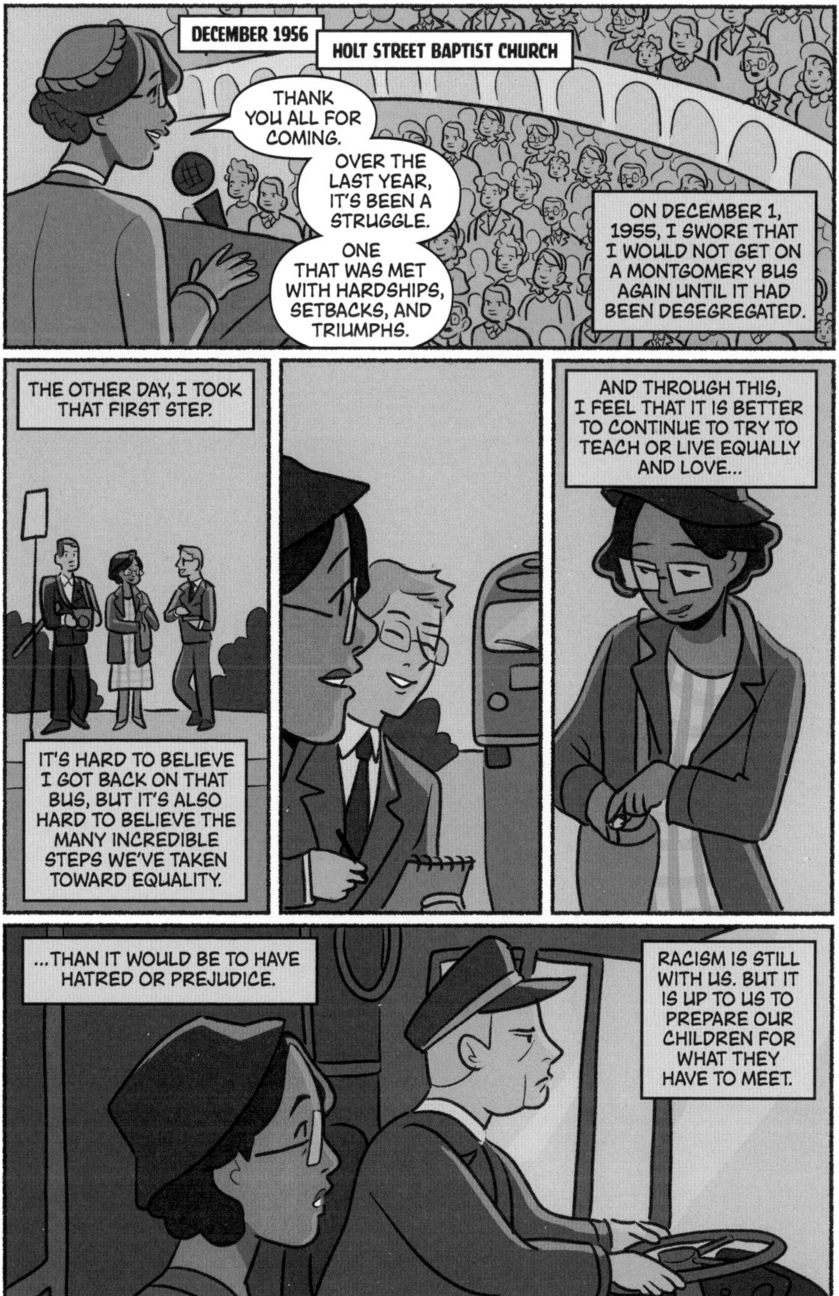
DECEMBER 1956
HOLT STREET BAPTIST CHURCH
THANK YOU ALL FOR COMING.
OVER THE LAST YEAR, IT'S BEEN A STRUGGLE.
ONE THAT WAS MET WITH HARDSHIPS, SETBACKS, AND TRIUMPHS.
ON DECEMBER 1, 1955, I SWORE THAT I WOULD NOT GET ON A MONTGOMERY BUS AGAIN UNTIL IT HAD BEEN DESEGREGATED.
THE OTHER DAY, I TOOK THAT FIRST STEP.
IT'S HARD TO BELIEVE I GOT BACK ON THAT BUS, BUT IT'S ALSO HARD TO BELIEVE THE MANY INCREDIBLE STEPS WE'VE TAKEN TOWARD EQUALITY.
AND THROUGH THIS, I FEEL THAT IT IS BETTER TO CONTINUE TO TRY TO TEACH OR LIVE EQUALLY AND LOVE...
...THAN IT WOULD BE TO HAVE HATRED OR PREJUDICE.
RACISM IS STILL WITH US. BUT IT IS UP TO US TO PREPARE OUR CHILDREN FOR WHAT THEY HAVE TO MEET.

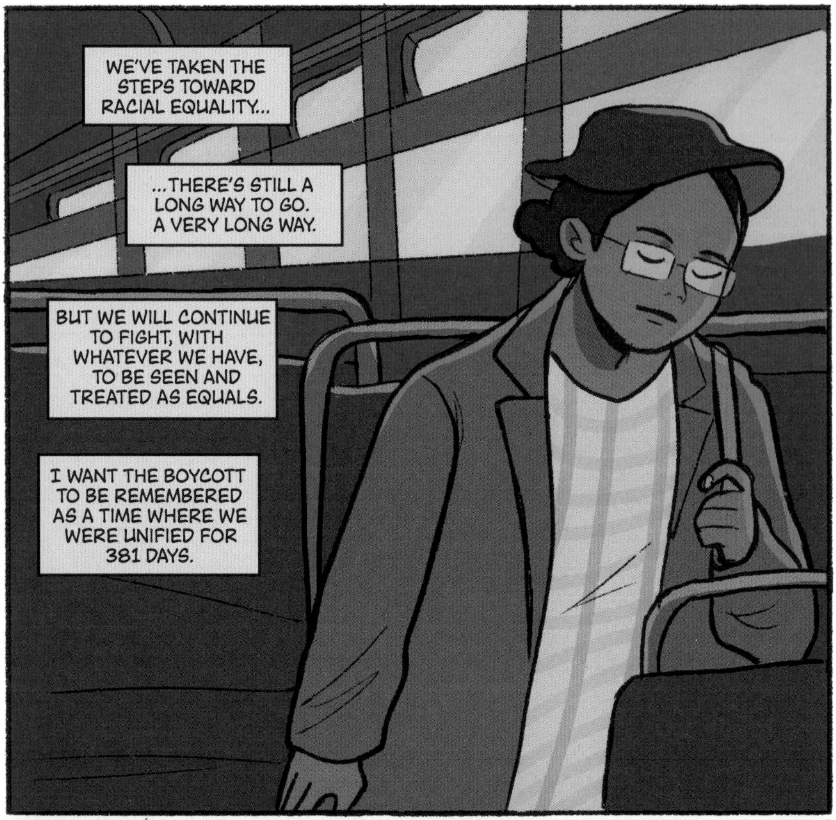
WE'VE TAKEN THE STEPS TOWARD RACIAL EQUALITY...
...THERE'S STILL A LONG WAY TO GO. A VERY LONG WAY.
BUT WE WILL CONTINUE TO FIGHT, WITH WHATEVER WE HAVE, TO BE SEEN AND TREATED AS EQUALS.
I WANT THE BOYCOTT TO BE REMEMBERED AS A TIME WHERE WE WERE UNIFIED FOR 381 DAYS.

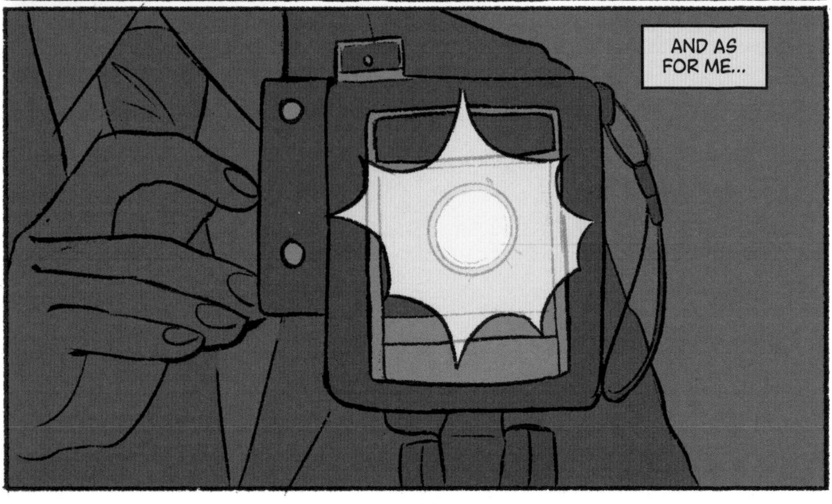
AND AS FOR ME...

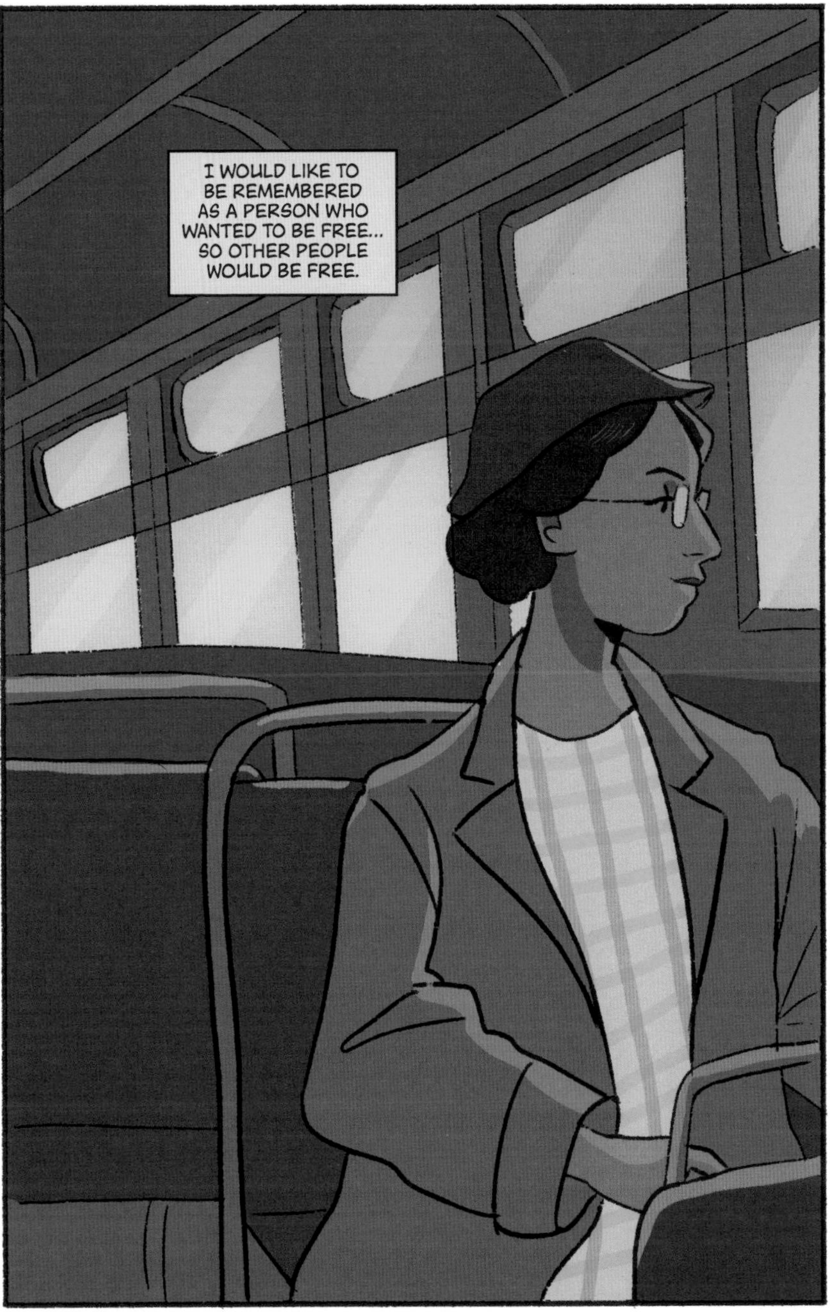
I WOULD LIKE TO BE REMEMBERED AS A PERSON WHO WANTED TO BE FREE... SO OTHER PEOPLE WOULD BE FREE.

Conclusion

After the Montgomery Bus Boycott, Rosa Parks moved out of the spotlight, but things were still hard for her and her family. Rosa and Raymond continued to receive threats and struggled to get any type of work. They had to make a tough decision: After living in Montgomery, Alabama, for most of their lives, Rosa, Raymond, and Rosa's mother, Leona, decided to move to Detroit, Michigan, to live near Rosa's brother, Sylvester McCauley.

The move from Montgomery was difficult, but it didn't stop Rosa from advocating for civil rights. Rosa worked with the local Detroit chapter of the NAACP and gave many speeches in churches and schools about her experiences. She walked in the March on Washington in 1963 and watched Martin Luther King Jr. give his "I Have a Dream" speech that same year. Two years later, she participated in the Selma to Montgomery March, a protest that helped allow Black people to vote.

In 1987, at seventy-four years old, she cofounded the Rosa and Raymond Parks Institute for Self-Development in Detroit with Elaine Eason Steele. The institute became a place to educate young people to better themselves and their community. The NAACP awarded Rosa the Spingarn Medal in 1979. She then received the Presidential Medal of Freedom in 1996 and the Congressional Gold Medal in 1999. She was named one of the most important people of the twentieth century in *Time* magazine. Rosa also wrote four books, including her 1992 memoir, with the help of author Jim Haskins, titled *Rosa Parks: My Story*.

On October 24, 2005, Rosa Parks died of natural causes at ninety-two. She was laid to rest in the Capitol building in Washington, DC, the first woman to have that honor. Rosa Parks spent her life fighting for civil rights—from standing up for herself on the bus to marching with thousands to help gain Black Americans the right to vote. Behind every movement, there's someone who lights the spark. Rosa lit the match when she stood her ground that day at the Cleveland Avenue bus stop. And the rest? Fireworks.

Timeline of Rosa Parks's Life

1913 — Rosa Louise McCauley is born in Tuskegee, Alabama

1932 — Marries Raymond Parks

1943 — Becomes secretary of the Montgomery chapter of the NAACP

1955 — Arrested for not giving her seat up to a white man; Montgomery Bus Boycott begins

— Rosa Parks's trial begins, and she's found guilty

1956 — In February, Martin Luther King Jr., Rosa Parks, E.D. Nixon, Jo Ann Robinson, and others are arrested for violating the state law against boycotting

— In November, US Supreme Court sides with Aurelia Browder in *Browder v. Gayle*, saying that segregation on buses is unconstitutional

1957 — Rosa, Raymond, and Leona move to Detroit

1965 — In March, Selma to Montgomery March begins

— President Lyndon B. Johnson signs the Voting Rights Act of 1965 into law

1975 — Rosa Parks returns for the 20th anniversary of the Montgomery Bus Boycott

1979 — The NAACP gives Rosa the Spingarn Medal

1996 — Receives the Presidential Medal of Freedom

1999 — Receives the Congressional Gold Medal of Honor

2005 — Dies of natural causes at age ninety-two

Bibliography

*Books for young readers

Brinkley, Douglas. *Rosa Parks: A Life.* New York: Penguin Books, 2005.

*Freedman, Russell. *Freedom Walkers: The Story of the Montgomery Bus Boycott.* New York: Holiday House, 2009.

*McDonough, Yona Zeldis. *Who Was Rosa Parks?* New York: Penguin Workshop, 2010.

"Montgomery Bus Boycott." History.com, A&E Networks, February 3, 2010. https://www.history.com/topics/black-history/montgomery-bus-boycott.

*Parks, Rosa, with Jim Haskins. *Rosa Parks: My Story.* New York: Dial Books, 1992.

*Pinkney, Andrea Davis, and Brian Pinkney. *Boycott Blues: How Rosa Parks Inspired a Nation.* New York: Greenwillow Books, 2008.

Robinson, Jo Ann, with David J. Garrow. *Montgomery Bus Boycott and the Women Who Started It: The Memoir of Jo Ann Gibson Robinson.* Knoxville, TN: University of Tennessee Press, 1987.

"Rosa Parks." Biography.com, A&E Networks, February 4, 2020. www.biography.com/activist/rosa-parks.

"Rosa Parks." History.com, A&E Networks, November 9, 2009. www.history.com/topics/black-history/rosa-parks.

*Summer, L.S. *Rosa Parks: Journey to Freedom.* North Mankato, MN: The Child's World, 2000.

*Time for Kids. *Heroes of Black History.* New York: Liberty Street (Time Inc. Books), 2017.

ABOUT THE CREATORS

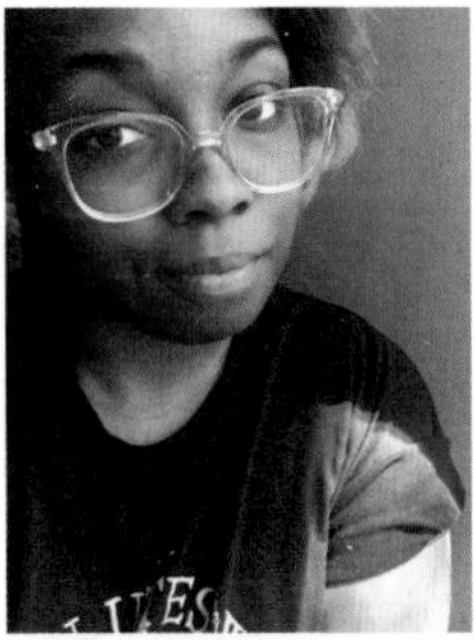

Insha Fitzpatrick is a New Jersey-based writer and editor. She's the founder of DIS/MEMBER, a horror genre website, and cowriter of middle-grade graphic novel series *Oh My Gods!* (Etch, 2021). Please talk to her about spooky movies, true crime, or Rod Serling's *Twilight Zone*.

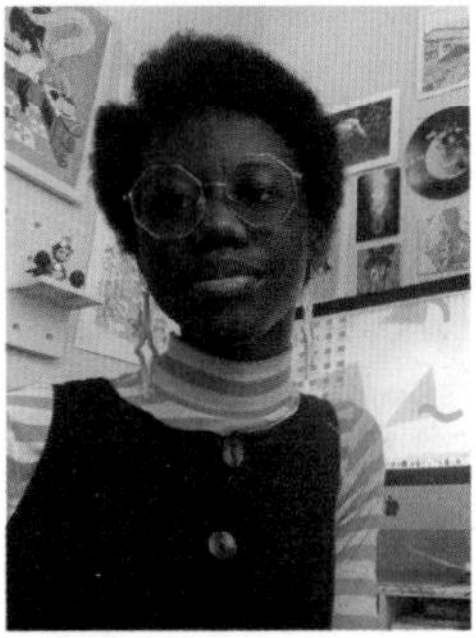

Abelle Hayford is a Ghanaian American illustrator, character designer, and color stylist. Their past clients include Warner Bros., *New York Times*, Penguin Random House, Simon & Schuster, and the *New Yorker*. Social media has played a huge role in Abelle's artistic growth, and they use their social media to share their art to others while also promoting other marginalized artists. In this effort, Abelle organized #Drawingwhileblack, a viral hashtag to celebrate and promote Black artists around the world!

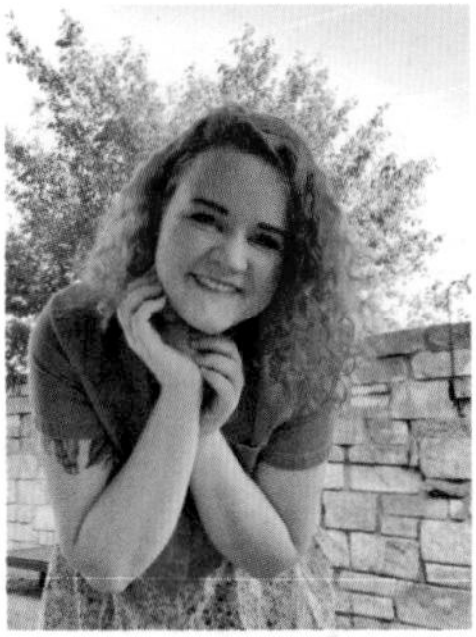

Hanna Schroy is an Austin-based cartoonist and illustrator. She is the creator of *Last Dance* (Iron Circus Comics, 2021) and a contributor in the anthology *Girls! Girls! Girls!* curated by Alex Perkins.